# Holt
# Middle School Math

## Chapter 2 Resource Book
## Course 2

**HOLT, RINEHART AND WINSTON**

A Harcourt Education Company

**Austin** • Orlando • Chicago • New York • Toronto • London • San Diego

Printed in the United States of America

ISBN 0-03-067941-9

1  2  3  4  5    082    05  04  03  02

# CONTENTS

## Blackline Masters

| | |
|---|---|
| Parent Letter | 1 |
| Are You Ready? Recording Sheet | 3 |
| Chapter 2 Planning and Pacing Guide | 5 |
| Section A Planner | 6 |
| Lesson 2-1 Exploration | 7 |
| Lesson 2-1 Exploration Recording Sheet | 8 |
| Lesson 2-1 Practice A, B, C | 9 |
| Lesson 2-1 Reteach | 12 |
| Lesson 2-1 Challenge | 13 |
| Lesson 2-1 Problem Solving | 14 |
| Lesson 2-1 Puzzles, Twisters & Teasers | 15 |
| Lesson 2-2 Exploration | 16 |
| Lesson 2-2 Exploration Recording Sheet | 17 |
| Lesson 2-2 Practice A, B, C | 18 |
| Lesson 2-2 Reteach | 21 |
| Lesson 2-2 Challenge | 22 |
| Lesson 2-2 Problem Solving | 23 |
| Lesson 2-2 Puzzles, Twisters & Teasers | 24 |
| Lesson 2-3 Exploration | 25 |
| Lesson 2-3 Exploration Recording Sheet | 26 |
| Lesson 2-3 Practice A, B, C | 27 |
| Lesson 2-3 Reteach | 30 |
| Lesson 2-3 Challenge | 31 |
| Lesson 2-3 Problem Solving | 32 |
| Lesson 2-3 Puzzles, Twisters & Teasers | 33 |
| Section B Planner | 34 |
| Lesson 2-4 Exploration | 35 |
| Lesson 2-4 Exploration Recording Sheet | 36 |
| Lesson 2-4 Practice A, B, C | 37 |
| Lesson 2-4 Reteach | 40 |
| Lesson 2-4 Challenge | 41 |
| Lesson 2-4 Problem Solving | 42 |
| Lesson 2-4 Puzzles, Twisters, & Teasers | 43 |
| Lesson 2-5 Exploration | 44 |
| Lesson 2-5 Exploration Recording Sheet | 45 |
| Lesson 2-5 Practice A, B, C | 46 |
| Lesson 2-5 Reteach | 49 |
| Lesson 2-5 Challenge | 50 |
| Lesson 2-5 Problem Solving | 51 |
| Lesson 2-5 Puzzles, Twisters & Teasers | 52 |
| Lesson 2-6 Exploration | 53 |
| Lesson 2-6 Exploration Recording Sheet | 54 |
| Lesson 2-6 Practice A, B, C | 55 |
| Lesson 2-6 Reteach | 58 |
| Lesson 2-6 Challenge | 59 |
| Lesson 2-6 Problem Solving | 60 |
| Lesson 2-6 Puzzles, Twisters & Teasers | 61 |
| Section C Planner | 62 |
| Lesson 2-7 Exploration | 63 |
| Lesson 2-7 Exploration Recording Sheet | 64 |
| Lesson 2-7 Practice A, B, C | 65 |
| Lesson 2-7 Reteach | 68 |
| Lesson 2-7 Challenge | 69 |
| Lesson 2-7 Problem Solving | 70 |
| Lesson 2-7 Puzzles, Twisters & Teasers | 71 |
| Lesson 2-8 Exploration | 72 |
| Lesson 2-8 Exploration Recording Sheet | 73 |
| Lesson 2-8 Practice A, B, C | 74 |
| Lesson 2-8 Reteach | 77 |
| Lesson 2-8 Challenge | 78 |
| Lesson 2-8 Problem Solving | 79 |
| Lesson 2-8 Puzzles, Twisters & Teasers | 80 |
| Lesson 2-9 Exploration | 81 |
| Lesson 2-9 Exploration Recording Sheet | 82 |
| Lesson 2-9 Practice A, B, C | 84 |
| Lesson 2-9 Reteach | 87 |
| Lesson 2-9 Challenge | 88 |
| Lesson 2-9 Problem Solving | 89 |
| Lesson 2-9 Puzzles, Twisters & Teasers | 90 |
| Lesson 2-10 Exploration | 91 |
| Lesson 2-10 Exploration Recording Sheet | 92 |
| Lesson 2-10 Practice A, B, C | 93 |
| Lesson 2-10 Reteach | 96 |
| Lesson 2-10 Challenge | 97 |

Holt Middle School Math    Course 2

# CONTENTS, *CONTINUED*

| | | | |
|---|---|---|---|
| Lesson 2-10 Problem Solving | 98 | **Transparencies** | |
| Lesson 2-10 Puzzles, Twisters & Teasers | 99 | Lesson 2-1 Daily Transparency | T1 |
| Lesson 2-11 Exploration | 100 | Lesson 2-1 Additional Examples Transparency | T2 |
| Lesson 2-11 Exploration Recording Sheet | 101 | Lesson 2-2 Daily Transparency | T4 |
| Lesson 2-11 Practice A, B, C | 102 | Lesson 2-2 Additional Examples Transparency | T5 |
| Lesson 2-11 Reteach | 105 | Lesson 2-3 Daily Transparency | T8 |
| Lesson 2-11 Challenge | 106 | Lesson 2-3 Teaching Transparency | T9 |
| Lesson 2-11 Problem Solving | 107 | Lesson 2-3 Additional Examples Transparency | T10 |
| Lesson 2-11 Puzzles, Twisters & Teasers | 108 | Lesson 2-4 Daily Transparency | T13 |
| Lesson 2-12 Exploration | 109 | Lesson 2-4 Additional Examples Transparency | T14 |
| Lesson 2-12 Exploration Recording Sheet | 110 | Lesson 2-5 Daily Transparency | T16 |
| Lesson 2-12 Practice A, B, C | 111 | Lesson 2-5 Additional Examples Transparency | T17 |
| Lesson 2-12 Reteach | 114 | Lesson 2-6 Daily Transparency | T19 |
| Lesson 2-12 Challenge | 115 | Lesson 2-6 Additional Examples Transparency | T20 |
| Lesson 2-12 Problem Solving | 116 | Lesson 2-7 Daily Transparency | T23 |
| Lesson 2-12 Puzzles, Twisters & Teasers | 117 | Lesson 2-7 Additional Examples Transparency | T24 |
| Chapter Review | 118 | Lesson 2-8 Daily Transparency | T26 |
| Project Recording Sheet | 121 | Lesson 2-8 Teaching Transparency | T27 |
| Project Teacher Support | 122 | Lesson 2-8 Additional Examples Transparency | T28 |
| List of Tools | 123 | Lesson 2-9 Daily Transparency | T30 |
| Teacher Tools | 124 | Lesson 2-9 Teaching Transparency | T31 |
| Answers to Blackline Masters | 130 | Lesson 2-9 Additional Examples Transparency | T32 |
| | | Lesson 2-10 Daily Transparency | T34 |
| | | Lesson 2-10 Teaching Transparency | T35 |
| | | Lesson 2-10 Additional Examples Transparency | T36 |
| | | Lesson 2-11 Daily Transparency | T39 |
| | | Lesson 2-11 Teaching Transparency | T40 |
| | | Lesson 2-11 Additional Examples Transparency | T41 |
| | | Lesson 2-12 Daily Transparency | T43 |
| | | Lesson 2-12 Teaching Transparency | T44 |
| | | Lesson 2-12 Additional Examples Transparency | T45 |

Holt Middle School Math   Course 2

# DESCRIPTION OF THIS BOOK

In order to make your planning easier, this Chapter Resource Book is organized by lessons. These materials are provided:

## Black Line Masters

1. *Parent letters*

   These letters describe the math the student will be studying in the chapter. Some worked out examples are provided for the parents.

2. *Recording Sheet for Are You Ready?*

   This is a recording sheet for the prechapter assessment that is in the student book.

3. *Chapter Planning and Pacing Guide*

   This is a copy of the Chapter Pacing Guide that is found in the Teacher's Edition.

4. *Section Planning Guides*

   These are copies of the Section Planning Guides that are found in the Teacher's Edition.

5. *Copy of the Explorations*

   These are copies of the Explorations that are shown in the Teacher's Edition. These are also available as transparencies. There is one for every lesson. The Explorations are alternative ways to teach the lesson.

6. *Recording Sheets for the Explorations*

   These are recording sheets for the student to use for the Explorations.

7. *Practice A, B, and C*

   There are three practice masters for every lesson. All of these reinforce the content of the lesson. Practice B is shown in the Teacher's Edition and is appropriate for the average student. It is also available as a workbook.

   Practice A is easier than Practice B, but still practices the content of the lesson. Practice C is more challenging than Practice B and extends the students' thinking.

8. *Reteach*

   There is a reteach master for every lesson. These provide an alternative way to teach the lesson concepts. Each of these masters is one or two pages long. These masters are shown in the Teacher's Edition.

9. *Challenge*

   There is a challenge master for every lesson that enhances critical thinking skills and extends the topic. These masters are shown in the Teacher's Edition.

10. *Problem Solving*

    There is a problem solving master for every lesson that provides practice in problem solving and provides opportunities for real world applications and interdisciplinary connections. These masters are shown in the Teacher's Edition.

11. *Puzzles, Twisters & Teasers*

    There is a master for every lesson that provides fun practice while reinforcing the content of the lesson.

**Holt Middle School Math   Course 2**

# DESCRIPTION OF THIS BOOK, *CONTINUED*

**12.** *Chapter Review*

There is a two- or three-page master for each chapter that reviews the content of the chapter. Each set of exercises indicates which lesson the set reviews.

**13.** *Project Recording Sheet*

There is a master for each chapter that the students can use to record their results for the chapter project.

**14.** *Teacher Support for Projects*

There is one page of teacher support for the chapter project.

**15.** *Teacher Tools*

Tools needed for any of the features in the student book, Teacher's Edition, and ancillaries in this CRB are provided.

These include such things as place value charts, number lines, and grid paper.

**16.** *Answers*

Answers are provided for all of the masters in the Chapter Resource Book.

**Transparencies**

**1.** *Daily Transparency*

These transparencies provide a Warm Up, Problem of the Day, and Lesson Quiz for every lesson.

**2.** *Additional Examples*

The Additional Examples from the Teacher's Edition are provided as transparencies for ease of use.

These include such things as place value charts, number lines, and grid paper.

**3.** *Teaching Transparencies*

Teaching Transparencies are provided as appropriate. These enhance lesson presentations. They include graphics from the student text and teacher tools.

Holt Middle School Math    Course 2

Date _____

Dear Family,

In this chapter students will learn about exponents, scientific notation, order of operations, divisibility rules, and finding prime factors. They will work with variables and algebraic expressions and learn how to solve equations.

Using **exponents** is an efficient way of expressing large numbers. Exponents typically appear in scientific work and publications.

An exponent tells how many times to multiply a number, the base, by itself.

$$\text{base} \longrightarrow \mathbf{5^2} \longleftarrow \text{exponent}$$

$5^2$ expresses **5 × 5.** The total value equals 25.

When dealing with very large numbers, **scientific notation,** a kind of shorthand, is used. In order to write a number in scientific notation:

1. Move the decimal point to create a number between 1 and 10.

2. Count the number of places you moved the decimal to create that number.

3. The number of places you moved the decimal is the power of 10 for that number.

In scientific notation the number 17,900,000 is expressed as:

$$1.79 \times 10^7$$

A **factor** is a number that is multiplied by another number to get a **product.**

A **prime number** has exactly two factors, one and the number itself. The number 11 is a **prime number** because there are only two factors, 11 and 1, which can be multiplied to get 11.

A **composite number** has more than two factors. The number 12 is a **composite number.** The factors of 12 are 12 and 1, 6 and 2 and 4 and 3. All composite numbers can be written as the product of prime factors. This is called the **prime factorization.**

Students will learn to use a factor tree to find the prime factorization of a number. The following example shows the **prime factorization** for 36.

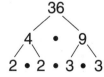

4 • 9    Write 36 as the product of two factors.

2 • 2 • 3 • 3    Continue factoring until all factors are prime.

1    **Holt Middle School Math   Course 2**

The prime factorization of 36 is $2 \cdot 2 \cdot 3 \cdot 3$. Using exponents, you can write this as $2^2 \cdot 3^2$.

This is an **algebraic expression.**

$$\text{variable} \longrightarrow \boldsymbol{n + 3} \longleftarrow \text{constant}$$

Students learn to find the value of an expression by replacing the variable with a number and using that number to compute the result.

**Find the value of $(n + 3) - 10$ when $n = 15$.**

$(15 + 3) - 10$
$\quad 18 \quad - 10 = 8$

When solving equations, we use the **order of operations,** a special set of rules to follow when there is more than one operation in the equation.

---

**1.** Perform the operations inside the parentheses.
**2.** Multiply and divide from left to right.
**3.** Add and subtract from left to right

---

**Solve $15(8 - 6)$**

        **1.** $8 - 6 = 2$
        **2.** $15 - 2 = 13$

**Solve $3(5) - 2$**

        **1.** $3 \times 5 = 15$
        **2.** $15 - 2 = 13.$

Addition and subtraction are **inverse,** or opposite operations. Multiplication and division are also **inverse** operations. When an equation involves addition, it can be solved by subtracting from both sides. That act of subtracting undoes the addition. The same is true for multiplication and division.

**Solve: $n + 7 = 11$**

        **1.** In the above equation, $n$ is added to 7.
        **2.** In order to solve for $n$, you subtract 7
           from both sides.
           $n + 7 - 7 = 11 - 7$
        **3.** $n = 4$

Visit www.parent.msm.HRW.com to find links to activities to do with your child.

**Holt Middle School Math   Course 2**

Name _____ Date _____ Class _____

**Are You Ready? Recording Sheet**
*Number Theory and Algebraic Reasoning*

**Choose the best term from the list to complete each sentence.**

division    factor    multiplication    place value    product    quotient

**1.** The operation that gives the quotient of two numbers is _____.

**2.** The _____ of the digit 3 in 4,903,672 is thousands.

**3.** A number that is multiplied by another number is called a _____.

**4.** The operation that gives the product of two numbers is _____.

**5.** In the equation 15 ÷ 3 = 5, the _____ is 5.

**Give the place value of the digit 4 in each number.**

**6.** 4,092        **7.** 608,241        **8.** 7,040,000        **9.** 4,556,890,100

_____      _____      _____      _____

**10.** 3,408,289        **11.** 34,506,123        **12.** 500,986,402        **13.** 3,540,277,009

_____      _____      _____      _____

**Find each product.**

**14.** $2 \cdot 2 \cdot 2$        **15.** $9 \cdot 9 \cdot 9 \cdot 9$        **16.** $14 \cdot 14 \cdot 14$        **17.** $10 \cdot 10 \cdot 10 \cdot 10$

_____      _____      _____      _____

**18.** $3 \cdot 3 \cdot 5 \cdot 5$        **19.** $2 \cdot 2 \cdot 5 \cdot 7$        **20.** $3 \cdot 3 \cdot 11 \cdot 11$        **21.** $5 \cdot 10 \cdot 10 \cdot 10$

_____      _____      _____      _____

**Find the first five multiples of each number.**

**22.** 2 _____        **23.** 9 _____

**24.** 15 _____        **25.** 1 _____

**26.** 101 _____        **27.** 54 _____

**28.** 326 _____        **29.** 1,024 _____

Holt Middle School Math   **Course 2**

# CHAPTER 2 Are You Ready? Recording Sheet *(continued)*
## *Number Theory and Algebraic Reasoning*

**List all the factors of each number.**

**30.** 8 _____

**31.** 22 _____

**32.** 36 _____

**33.** 50 _____

**34.** 108 _____

**35.** 84 _____

**36.** 256 _____

**37.** 630 _____

_____

Holt Middle School Math    Course 2

# Planning and Pacing Guide
## Number Theory and Algebraic Reasoning

| Section 2A | Section 2B | Section 2C |
|---|---|---|
| **Exponents** | **Factors and Multiples** | **Beginning Algebra** |
| Lesson 2-1<br>Exponents | Hands-On Lab 2B<br>Divisibility | Lesson 2-7<br>Variables and Algebraic Expressions |
| Lesson 2-2<br>Powers of Ten and Scientific Notation | Lesson 2-4<br>Prime Factorization | Lesson 2-8<br>Translate Words into Math |
| Technology Lab 2A<br>Scientific Notation with a Calculator | Lesson 2-5<br>Greatest Common Factor | Lesson 2-9<br>Combining Like Terms |
| Lesson 2-3<br>Order of Operations | Lesson 2-6<br>Least Common Multiple | Lesson 2-10<br>Equations and Their Solutions |
| | | Hands-On Lab 2C<br>Model Equations |
| | | Lesson 2-11<br>Solving Equations by Adding or Subtracting |
| | | Lesson 2-12<br>Solving Equations by Multiplying or Dividing |

## Pacing Options for 45-minute Classes
## Hands-on Labs and Extensions

| DAY 15<br>Lesson 2-1 | DAY 16<br>Lesson 2-2 | DAY 17<br>Technology Lab 2A | DAY 18<br>Lesson 2-3 | DAY 19<br>Mid-Chapter Quiz<br>Hands-On Lab 2B |
|---|---|---|---|---|
| DAY 20<br>Lesson 2-4 | DAY 21<br>Lesson 2-5 | DAY 22<br>Lesson 2-6 | DAY 23<br>Mid-Chapter Quiz<br>Lesson 2-7 | DAY 24<br>Lesson 2-8 |
| DAY 25<br>Lesson 2-9 | DAY 26<br>Lesson 2-10 | DAY 27<br>Hands-On Lab 2C | DAY 28<br>Lesson 2-11 | DAY 29<br>Lesson 2-12 |
| DAY 30<br>Chapter 2 Review | DAY 31<br>Chapter 2 Assessment | | | |

## Pacing Options for 90-minute Classes
## Hands-on Labs and Extensions

| DAY 7<br>Chapter 1 Review<br>Lesson 2-1 | DAY 8<br>Chapter 1 Assessment<br>Lesson 2-2 | DAY 9<br>Technology Lab 2A<br>Lesson 2-3 | DAY 10<br>Mid-Chapter Quiz<br>Hands-On Lab 2B<br>Lesson 2-4 | DAY 11<br>Lesson 2-5<br>Lesson 2-6 |
|---|---|---|---|---|
| DAY 12<br>Mid-Chapter Quiz<br>Lesson 2-7<br>Lesson 2-8 | DAY 13<br>Lesson 2-9<br>Lesson 2-10 | DAY 14<br>Hands-On Lab 2C<br>Lesson 2-11 | DAY 15<br>Lesson 2-12<br>Chapter 2 Review | DAY 16<br>Chapter 2 Assessment<br>Lesson 3-1 |

5          Holt Middle School Math   Course 2

# Section A Planner
## *Exponents*

| Lesson | Materials | Resources |
|---|---|---|
| **Lesson 2-1**<br>Exponents<br>NCTM: Number and Operations<br>Understand numbers (See p. T00.)<br>• Recognize and appropriately use exponential notation. | **Optional**<br>10-by-10 grids p. 00 CRB, MK<br>Calculators | • *Chapter 2 Resource Book,* pp. 00–00<br>• Daily Transparency, TXX CRB<br>• Additional Examples Transparency, TXX CRB<br>• *Alternate Openers: Explorations,* p. 10 |
| **Lesson 2-2**<br>Powers of Ten and Scientific Notation<br>NCTM: Number and Operations<br>Understand numbers (See p. T00.)<br>• Recognize and appropriately use exponential and scientific notation. | **Optional**<br>Calculators | • *Chapter 2 Resource Book,* pp. 00–00<br>• Daily Transparency, TXX CRB<br>• Additional Examples Transparency, TXX CRB<br>• *Alternate Openers: Explorations,* p. 11 |
| **Technology Lab 2A**<br>Scientific Notation with a Calculator<br>NCTM: Number and Operations<br>Understand meanings (See p. T00.)<br>• Understand the meanings and effects of arithmetic operations. | **Required**<br>Calculators | •*Technology Lab Activities,* pp. 00 |
| **Lesson 2-3**<br>Order of Operations<br>NCTM: Number and Operations<br>Understand meanings (See p. T00.)<br>• Understand the meanings and effects of arithmetic operations. | **Optional**<br>Calculators<br>Recording Sheet for Reaching All Learners p. 00 CRB<br>Teaching Transparency TXX CRB | • *Chapter 2 Resource Book,* pp. 00–00<br>• Daily Transparency, TXX CRB<br>• Additional Examples Transparency, TXX CRB<br>• *Alternate Openers: Explorations,* p. 12 |
| **Section 2A Assessment** | | • Mid-Chapter Quiz, SE p. 74<br>• Section 2A Quiz, AR p. 8<br>• *Test and Practice Generator* CD-ROM |

**SE** = Student Edition     **TE** = Teacher's Edition     **AR** = Assessment Resources
**CRB** = Chapter Resource Book     **MK** = Manipulatives Kit

# EXPLORATION

## 2-1 Exponents

You can multiply $5 \cdot 5 \cdot 5 \cdot 5 \cdot 5 \cdot 5$ using exponents and a calculator.

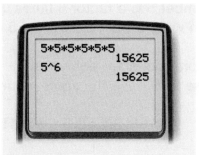

The number 5 is a factor 6 times, so you can write $5 \cdot 5 \cdot 5 \cdot 5 \cdot 5 \cdot 5$ as $5^6$.

The expressions are equivalent because they have the same value.

$$5 \cdot 5 \cdot 5 \cdot 5 \cdot 5 \cdot 5 = 15{,}625 \text{ and } 5^6 = 15{,}625$$

**Guess the missing exponent in each statement. Use a calculator after each guess to check your answer.**

**1.** $3^{\square} = 729$          **2.** $2^{\square} = 4{,}096$

**3.** $9^{\square} = 4{,}782{,}969$      **4.** $4^{\square} = 1{,}024$

## Think and Discuss

**5. Describe** the strategies you used to find the missing exponents.

**6. Explain** how you can find the value of $2^{11}$ if you know that $2^{10} = 1{,}024$.

**This page is available as a transparency.**

Holt Middle School Math   Course 2

## Exploration Recording Sheet

*Exponents*

You can multiply $5 \cdot 5 \cdot 5 \cdot 5 \cdot 5 \cdot 5$ using exponents and a calculator. The number 5 is a factor 6 times, so you can write $5 \cdot 5 \cdot 5 \cdot 5 \cdot 5 \cdot 5$ as $5^6$.
The expressions are equivalent because they have the same value.

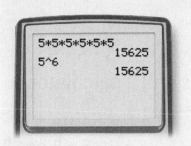

$$5 \cdot 5 \cdot 5 \cdot 5 \cdot 5 \cdot 5 = 15{,}625 \text{ and } 5^6 = 15{,}625$$

**Guess the missing exponent in each statement. Use a calculator after each guess to check your answer.**

1. $3^\square = 729$ _____

2. $2^\square = 4{,}096$ _____

3. $9^\square = 4{,}782{,}969$ _____

4. $4^\square = 1{,}024$ _____

## Think and Discuss

5. **Describe** the strategies you used to find the missing exponents.

_____

_____

_____

6. **Explain** how you can find the value of $2^{11}$ if you know that $2^{10} = 1{,}024$.

_____

_____

_____

**Holt Middle School Math**

## LESSON 2-1 Practice A
### Exponents

**Multiply.**

**1.** $4^2$

**2.** $2^3$

**3.** $6^2$

$4 \cdot 4 =$ _____

__ $\cdot$ __ $\cdot$ __ = ____

__ $\cdot$ __ = ____

**4.** $9^2$

**5.** $4^3$

**6.** $3^5$

**7.** $7^0$

_____

_____

_____

_____

**8.** $10^2$

**9.** $3^4$

**10.** $9^1$

**11.** $2^5$

_____

_____

_____

_____

**Use an exponent and the given base to write each number.**

**12.** 25, base 5

**13.** 3, base 3

**14.** 8, base 2

**15.** 1, base 4

_____

_____

_____

_____

**16.** 81, base 9

**17.** 64, base 4

**18.** 64, base 8

**19.** 9, base 3

_____

_____

_____

_____

**20.** 36, base 6

**21.** 16, base 2

**22.** 27, base 3

**23.** 400, base 20

_____

_____

_____

_____

**24.** The first day, Jessie has $2. The second day, she has twice as much money as the first day. The third day, she has twice as much money as the second day. Write the amount of money she has on the third day in exponential form. Then write the amount in standard form.

_____

**25.** Kevin runs 5 miles on Monday. The total number of miles he runs that week is 5 times the number of miles he runs on Monday. How many miles does Kevin run that week?

_____

Holt Middle School Math   Course 2

Name _____ Date _____ Class _____

## LESSON 2-1 Practice B
### Exponents

**Find each value.**

**1.** $5^2$      **2.** $2^4$      **3.** $3^3$      **4.** $7^2$

_____    _____    _____    _____

**5.** $4^4$      **6.** $12^2$      **7.** $10^3$      **8.** $11^1$

_____    _____    _____    _____

**9.** $1^6$      **10.** $20^2$      **11.** $6^3$      **12.** $7^3$

_____    _____    _____    _____

**Write each number using an exponent and the given base.**

**13.** 16, base 4    **14.** 25, base 25    **15.** 100, base 10    **16.** 125, base 5

_____    _____    _____    _____

**17.** 32, base 2    **18.** 243, base 3    **19.** 900, base 30    **20.** 121, base 11

_____    _____    _____    _____

**21.** 3,600, base 60    **22.** 256, base 4    **23.** 512, base 8    **24.** 196, base 14

_____    _____    _____    _____

**25.** Damon has 4 times as many stamps as Julia. Julia has 4 times as many stamps as Claire. Claire has 4 stamps. Write the number of stamps Damon has in both exponential form and standard form.

_____

**26.** Holly starts a jump rope exercise program. She jumps rope for 3 minutes the first week. In the second week, she triples the time she jumps. In the third week, she triples the time of the second week, and in the fourth week, she triples the time of the third week. How many minutes does she jump rope during the fourth week?

_____

Holt Middle School Math   Course 2

Name _____ Date _____ Class _____

# Practice C
### *Exponents*

**Find each value.**

**1.** $3^8$

**2.** $7^5$

**3.** $50^2$

_____

_____

_____

**4.** $2^3 + 7^2$

**5.** $4^2 + 5^3$

**6.** $6^1 + 8^2$

_____

_____

_____

**7.** $15^0 + 13^2$

**8.** $5^3 - 10^2$

**9.** $10^3 - 12^2$

_____

_____

_____

**10.** $2^4 + 3^3 - 1^5$

**11.** $4^3 - 6^2 + 9^2$

**12.** $4^0 + 11^2 - 7^0$

_____

_____

_____

**Write each number using an exponent and the given base.**

**13.** 343, base 7

**14.** 625, base 5

**15.** 1,728, base 12

_____

_____

_____

**16.** 225, base 15

**17.** 1,000,000, base 100

**18.** 1,225, base 35

_____

_____

_____

**19.** 6,561, base 9

**20.** 2,187, base 3

**21.** 8,000, base 20

_____

_____

_____

**22.** Jacob has 7 times as many postcards as Austin has. Austin has
7 times as many postcards as Angela has. Angela has 7 times
as many postcards as Samuel has. Samuel has 7 postcards.
Write the number of postcards Jacob has in both exponential
form and standard form.

_____

Holt Middle School Math    Course 2

# LESSON 2-1 Reteach
## *Exponents*

The exponent tells you how many times to multiply the base by itself.

base ———————→ $3^4$ ←——————— exponent

• To find $3^4$, multiply the base (3) times itself 4 times.

$$3^4 = 3 \cdot 3 \cdot 3 \cdot 3 = 81$$

To multiply, say to yourself:
3 times 3 is 9
9 times 3 is 27
27 times 3 is 81

**Find each value.**

**1.** $4^3 =$ _____ • _____ • _____ = 64

**2.** $1^5 =$ _____ • _____ • _____ • _____ • _____ = _____

**3.** $5^2$       **4.** $2^3$       **5.** $3^3$       **6.** $6^2$

_____    _____    _____    _____

**7.** $8^2$       **8.** $4^1$       **9.** $5^3$       **10.** $2^4$

_____    _____    _____    _____

• You can write 64 using an exponent with the base 8.

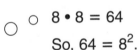

$8 \cdot 8 = 64$
So, $64 = 8^2$.

Think: How many times must you multiply 8 times itself to get a product of 64?

**Write each number using an exponent and the given base.**

**11.** 216, base 6: = _____ and $36 \cdot 6 =$ _____ so, 216 = _____.

**12.** 16, base 4      **13.** 8, base 2      **14.** 9, base 3

_____      _____      _____

**15.** 81, base 9      **16.** 27, base 3      **17.** 49, base 7

_____      _____      _____

Holt Middle School Math   Course 2

Name _____ Date _____ Class _____

# Challenge
## *Money Grows*

If an investment of $50 doubles in value, your investment will be
worth $50 • 2 = $100.

If it doubles again, your investment will be worth $50 • 2 • 2 = $200.
You can also write this as $50 • $2^2$ = $200.

If your money doubles a third time, it will be worth $50 • $2^3$ = $400.

**Write the correct answer.**

1. If you invest $400, how much will it
   be worth if it doubles in value twice?

   _____

2. If an investment of $550 doubles in
   value twice, how much will it be
   worth?

   _____

3. If you invest $75, how much will it be
   worth if it doubles in value 4 times?

   _____

4. If you invest $125, how much will it be
   worth if it doubles in value 4 times?

   _____

5. If an investment of $75 triples in
   value 3 times, how much will it be
   worth?

   _____

6. If an investment of $125 triples in
   value 4 times, how much will it be
   worth?

   _____

When Jasmine turned 13, she started saving $5 per month until she
turned 18. She then invested her total savings so that it doubled in
value every 7 years.

7. How much money did Jasmine save by the time she turned 18? _____

8. How many times will her investment double from age 18 to age 60? _____

9. How much will Jasmine's investment be worth when she turns 60? _____

When Jake turned 13, he started saving $1.50 per week until he
turned 19. He then invested his total savings so that it tripled in
value every 12 years.

10. How much money did Jake save by the time he turned 19? _____

11. How many times will his investment triple from age 19 to age 55? _____

12. How much will Jake's investment be worth when he turns 55? _____

Holt Middle School Math    Course 2

Name _____ Date _____ Class _____

# Problem Solving
## *Exponents*

**Write the correct answer.**

1. The cells of the bacteria *E. coli* can double every 20 minutes. If you begin with a single cell, how many cells can there be after 4 hours?

_____

2. The population of metropolitan Orlando, Florida, has doubled about every 16 years since 1960. In 2000, the population was 1,644,561. At this doubling rate, what could the population be in 2048?

_____

3. A prizewinner can choose Prize A, $2,000 per year for 15 years, or Prize B, 3 cents the first year, with the amount tripling each year through the fifteenth year. Which prize is more valuable? How much is it worth?

_____

4. Maria had triplets. Each of her 3 children had triplets. If the pattern continued for 2 more generations, how many great-great-grandchildren would Maria have?

_____

**Choose the letter for the best answer.**

5. A theory states that the CPU clock speed in a computer doubles every 18 months. If the clock speed was 33 MHz in 1991, how can you use exponents to find out how fast the clock speed is after doubling 3 times?

   A $33^3$         C $2^3 \cdot 33$

   B $3^2 \cdot 33$    D $33^2$

6. The classroom is a square with a side length of 13 feet and an area of 169 square feet. How can you write the area in exponential form?

   F $2^{13}$         H $3^{13}$

   G $13^2$          J $13^3$

7. In 2000, Wake County, North Carolina, had a population of 610,284. This is about twice the population in 1980. If the county grows at the same rate every 20 years, what will its population be in 2040?

   A 915,426        C 1,830,852

   B 1,220,568      D 2,441,136

8. The number of cells of a certain type of bacteria doubles every 45 minutes. If you begin with a single cell, how many cells could there be after 6 hours?

   F 64             H 360

   G 256            J 540

Holt Middle School Math   Course 2

Name _____ Date _____ Class _____

## Puzzles, Twisters & Teasers

### Explore Your Power Base!

**Why was the computer tired when it got home?**

To find out, solve each problem. Write the letter on the line above the correct answer at the bottom of the page. Each answer must match exactly. Some letters will not be used.

E $\quad 3^4 =$ _____

T $\quad$ 49, base 7 = _____

K $\quad 10^3 =$ _____

B $\quad$ 81, base 9 = _____

I $\quad 2^6 =$ _____

D $\quad 5^2 =$ _____

W $\quad 18^1 =$ _____

C $\quad$ 25, base 5 = _____

A $\quad$ 27, base 3 = _____

H $\quad 14^0 =$ _____

V $\quad 12^2 =$ _____

R $\quad$ 256, base 4 = _____

O $\quad$ 216, base 6 = _____

U $\quad 5^3 =$ _____

S $\quad 6^2 =$ _____

___  ___  ___  ___  ___  ___  ___  ___  ___  ___  ___  ___
$9^2$   81   $5^2$   $3^3$   125   36   81   64   $7^2$   1   $3^3$   25

___  ___  ___  ___  ___  ___  ___  ___  ___  ___
$3^3$   1   $3^3$   $4^4$   25   25   $4^4$   64   144   81

Holt Middle School Math   Course 2

# 2-2 Powers of Ten and Scientific Notation

**1.** Complete the table and look for a pattern.

| Power of 10 | Factors | Product |
|---|---|---|
| $10^1$ | 10 | 10 |
| $10^2$ | $10 \cdot 10$ | 100 |
| $10^3$ | $10 \cdot 10 \cdot 10$ | 1,000 |
| $10^4$ | | |
| $10^5$ | | |
| $10^6$ | | |
| $10^9$ | | |

**2.** Use the pattern you observed in the table to write 10,000,000 as a power of 10.

## Think and Discuss

**3. Describe** the pattern you observed in the table.

**4. Explain** how you know that $100,000 = 10^5$ is a true statement.

**This page is available as a transparency.**

Holt Middle School Math   Course 2

# Exploration Recording Sheet

*Powers of Ten and Scientific Notation*

**1.** Complete the table and look for a pattern.

| Power of 10 | Factors | Product |
|---|---|---|
| $10^1$ | 10 | 10 |
| $10^2$ | 10 · 10 | 100 |
| $10^3$ | 10 · 10 · 10 | 1,000 |
| $10^4$ | | |
| $10^5$ | | |
| $10^6$ | | |
| $10^9$ | | |

**2.** Use the pattern you observed in the table to write 10,000,000 as a power of 10.

_____

## Think and Discuss

**3. Describe** the pattern you observed in the table.

_____

_____

**4. Explain** how you know that $100,000 = 10^5$ is a true statement.

_____

_____

Holt Middle School Math    Course 2

Name _____ Date _____ Class _____

**Choose the letter for the best answer.**

1. $4 \cdot 10^2$
   - A  4
   - B  40
   - C  400
   - D  100

2. $16 \cdot 10^0$
   - F  1600
   - G  16
   - H  10
   - J  0

3. $9 \cdot 10^3$
   - A  9,000
   - B  900
   - C  90
   - D  9

4. $17 \cdot 10^1$
   - F  1.7
   - G  17
   - H  170
   - J  1700

**Multiply.**

5. $23 \cdot 10^2$

6. $15 \cdot 10^4$

7. $30 \cdot 10^2$

8. $28 \cdot 10^3$

_____   _____   _____   _____

9. $132 \cdot 10^2$

10. $201 \cdot 10^3$

11. $456 \cdot 10^2$

12. $108 \cdot 10^4$

_____   _____   _____   _____

**Write the number in scientific notation.**

13. 56,000

14. 306,000

15. 8,000,000

16. 7,200,000

_____   _____   _____   _____

17. 14,000,000

18. 41.00

19. 2,144,000

20. $20.3 \cdot 10^5$

_____   _____   _____   _____

21. Lake Huron covers an area of about 23,000 square miles. Write this number in scientific notation.

_____

22. The planet Mercury is about $3.6 \times 10^7$ miles from the sun. Write this number in standard form.

_____

Name _____ Date _____ Class _____

*Powers of Ten and Scientific Notation*

**Multiply.**

**1.** $6 \cdot 10^3$
**2.** $22 \cdot 10^1$
**3.** $8 \cdot 10^2$
**4.** $18 \cdot 10^0$

_____  _____  _____  _____

**5.** $70 \cdot 10^2$
**6.** $25 \cdot 10^3$
**7.** $3 \cdot 10^4$
**8.** $180 \cdot 10^3$

_____  _____  _____  _____

**Find each product.**

**9.** $84 \cdot 10^4$
**10.** $315 \cdot 10^2$
**11.** $210 \cdot 10^3$
**12.** $1{,}004 \cdot 10^3$

_____  _____  _____  _____

**13.** $1{,}764 \cdot 10^1$
**14.** $856 \cdot 10^0$
**15.** $4{,}055 \cdot 10^3$
**16.** $716 \cdot 10^4$

_____  _____  _____  _____

**Write each number in scientific notation.**

**17.** 34,000
**18.** 7,700
**19.** 2,100,000
**20.** 404,000

_____  _____  _____  _____

**21.** 21,000,000
**22.** 612.00
**23.** 3,001,000
**24.** $62.13 \cdot 10^4$

_____  _____  _____  _____

**25.** Lake Superior covers an area of about 31,700 square miles. Write this number in scientific notation.

_____

**26.** Mars is about $1.42 \cdot 10^8$ miles from the sun. Write this number in standard form.

_____

**27.** In 1999, the population of China was about $1.25 \cdot 10^9$. What was the population of China written in standard form?

_____

**28.** A scientist estimates there are 4,800,000 bacteria in a test tube. How does she record the number using scientific notation?

_____

Holt Middle School Math   Course 2

Name _____ Date _____ Class _____

## Practice C
### *Powers of Ten and Scientific Notation*

**Multiply.**

**1.** $5 \cdot 10^3$      **2.** $471 \cdot 10^2$      **3.** $39.5 \cdot 10^1$      **4.** $200 \cdot 10^5$

_____   _____   _____   _____

**5.** $7{,}025 \cdot 10^0$      **6.** $5.7 \cdot 10^6$      **7.** $66.25 \cdot 10^4$      **8.** $9.01 \cdot 10^9$

_____   _____   _____   _____

**Write each number in scientific notation.**

**9.** 25,000      **10.** 9,900      **11.** 9,700,000      **12.** $95.6 \cdot 10^8$

_____   _____   _____   _____

**13.** 23,000,000,000    **14.** 110.00      **15.** $301.9 \cdot 10^5$      **16.** $73.55 \cdot 10^4$

_____   _____   _____   _____

**Write the missing number or numbers.**

**17.** $1.23 \times 10^? = 12{,}300$      **18.** $8.3 \times 10^5 = ?$      **19.** $112{,}000{,}000 = ? \times 10^8$

_____   _____   _____

**20.** $410{,}000 = ? \times 10^5$      **21.** $7.7 \times 10^7 = ?$      **22.** $2{,}950{,}000 = 2.95 \times 10^?$

_____   _____   _____

**23.** The Caspian Sea covers an area of about 143,250 square
miles. Write this number in scientific notation.

_____

**24.** The distance between Jupiter and Saturn is about $4.03 \times 10^8$
miles. Write this number in standard form.

_____

**25.** In 1999, the population of the world was about $5.996 \times 10^9$.
What was the population in standard form?

_____

**26.** A scientist estimates there are 37,000,000 bacteria in a petri
dish. He records the number using scientific notation. What does
he write?

_____

**Holt Middle School Math**   **Course 2**

Name _____ Date _____ Class _____

# Reteach
## *Powers of Ten and Scientific Notation*

To multiply by a power of 10, use the exponent to find the number of zeros in the product.

• Multiply $42 \cdot 10^4$.

$$42 \cdot 10^4 = 420,000$$

> The exponent **4** tells you to write **4** zeros after 42 in the product.

**Find each product.**

**1.** $84 \cdot 10^3$

The product should have _____ zeros.

$84 \cdot 10^3 =$ _____

**2.** $61 \cdot 10^5$

The product should have _____ zeros.

$61 \cdot 10^5 =$ _____

**3.** $22 \cdot 10^6$      **4.** $753 \cdot 10^3$      **5.** $825 \cdot 10^2$      **6.** $123 \cdot 10^1$

_____      _____      _____      _____

• Write 926,000 in scientific notation.

First, write the digits before the zeros as a number greater than or equal to 1 and less than 10. The number must have only 1 digit to the left of the decimal point. That digit cannot be zero.

0 1 2 3 4 5 6 7 8 9 10

Think: 9.26 is greater than 1 and less than 10.

Then multiply 9.26 by the power of 10 that gives 926,000 as the product.

$$9\,2\,6\,0\,0\,0 = 9.26 \times 10^5$$

> The decimal point moves **5** places so the exponent is **5**.

**Write each number in scientific notation.**

**7.** 5,100

The decimal point moves _____ places.

$5,100 =$ _____ . _____ $\times 10^-$

**8.** 1,840,000

The decimal point moves _____ places.

$1,840,000 =$ _____ . _____ $\times 10^-$

**9.** 641,000      **10.** 47,300      **11.** 8,250,000      **12.** 703,000

_____      _____      _____      _____

Holt Middle School Math   **Course 2**

# Challenge
## 2-2 Computer Bytes

LESSON

Each byte in a computer's memory represents about one character. The major units of computer memory are kilobytes (KB), megabytes (MB), and gigabytes (GB).

| | |
|---|---|
| 1 kilobyte   = 1,000 bytes | 1 KB = 1,000 bytes |
| 1 megabyte  = 1,000 kilobytes | 1 MG = 1,000 KB |
| 1 gigabyte   = 1,000 megabytes | 1 GB = 1,000 MB |

**Write your answers using scientific notation.**

**1.** In 1984, many personal computers had 64 KB of active (RAM) memory. How many bytes does this represent?

**2.** In 1992, many personal computers had 40 MB of hard drive memory. How many bytes does this represent?

**3.** In 1997, many personal computers had 1 GB of hard drive memory. How many bytes does this represent?

**4.** By 2001, many personal computers had 20 GB of hard drive memory. How many bytes does this represent?

Ming saved his computer files on floppy disks. Each disk holds up to 1.44 MB of memory. He used these disks to transfer his files to another computer.

**5.** How many bytes could each floppy disk hold?

**6.** Ming's new computer has 12 GB of memory. How many disks could he transfer if each disk held 1.2 MB?

Rachel decided to back up her hard drive's computer files by copying them onto compact disks (CDs). Each CD can hold up to 650 MB of memory, but Rachel saves only 600 MB on each.

**7.** How many bytes could each CD potentially hold?

**8.** If Rachel backs up 6 GB of memory, how many bytes of memory will she need?

**Holt Middle School Math   Course 2**

Name _____ Date _____ Class _____

**Write the correct answer.**

1. Earth is about 150,000,000 kilometers from the sun. Write this distance in scientific notation.

_____

2. The planet Neptune is about $4.5 \times 10^9$ kilometers from the sun. Write this distance in standard form.

_____

3. In 1999, the U.S. federal debt was about $5 trillion, 600 billion. Write the amount of the debt in standard form and in scientific notation.

_____

_____

4. Canada is about $1.0 \times 10^7$ square kilometers in size. Brazil is about 8,500,000 square kilometers in size. Which country has a greater area?

_____

_____

**Choose the letter for the best answer.**

5. China's population in 2001 was approximately 1,273,000,000. Mexico's population for the same year was about $1.02 \times 10^8$. How much greater was China's population than Mexico's?

   A 1,375,000,000
   B 1,274,020,000
   C 1,171,000,000
   D 102,000,000

6. In mid-2001, the world population was approximately $6.137 \times 10^9$. By 2050, the population is projected to be $9.036 \times 10^9$. By how much will world population increase?

   F 151,730,000
   G 289,900,000
   H 1,517,300,000
   J 2,899,000,000

7. The Alpha Centauri star system is about 4.3 light-years from Earth. One light-year, the distance light travels in 1 year, is about 6 trillion miles. About how many miles away from Earth is Alpha Centauri?

   A $2.58 \times 10^{13}$ miles
   B $6 \times 10^{13}$ miles
   C $1.03 \times 10^{12}$ miles
   D $2.58 \times 10^9$ miles

8. In the fall of 2001, students in Columbia, South Carolina, raised $440,000 to buy a new fire truck for New York City. If the money had been collected in pennies, how many pennies would that have been?

   F $4.4 \times 10^6$
   G $4.4 \times 10^5$
   H $4.4 \times 10^7$
   J $4.4\ 3\ 10^8$

Holt Middle School Math   Course 2

## Puzzles, Twisters & Teasers

**LESSON 2-2** *Oh, the Power of Tens!*

Substitute the correct number for the letter or letters in each equation. Use your answers to solve the riddle.

**1.** $24{,}500 = 2.45 \times 10^E$ _____

**2.** $280{,}000 = 2.8 \times 10^P$ _____

**3.** $592{,}000 = I \times 10^5$ _____

**4.** $16{,}800 = C \times 10^4$ _____

**5.** $5.4 \times 10^H = 540{,}000{,}000$ _____

**6.** $24{,}400{,}000 = S \times 10^A$ _____

What's a Martian's favorite snack?

___  ___  ___  ___  ___  ___  ___  ___  ___  ___
2.44   5    7   1.68   4    1.68   8   5.92   5   2.44

Holt Middle School Math   Course 2

# 2-3 Order of Operations

Many calculators are programmed to compute in a certain order, called the *order of operations*.

**1.** Determine the order the calculator follows for each expression in the window.

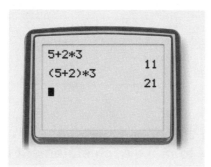

Use the necessary operation symbols +, −, ×, and ÷ and the grouping symbols ) and ( to make each statement true. Verify with your calculator.

**2.** 4  3  6 = 7

**3.** 4  3  6 = 6

**4.** 4  3  6 = 22

**5.** 4  3  6 = 42

**6.** 4  3  6 = 2

**7.** 6  3  4 = 8

## Think and Discuss

**8. Explain** how the grouping symbols ) and ( are used in the order of operations.

**9. Describe** the order of operations in your own words.

**This page is available as a transparency.**

Name _____ Date _____ Class _____

# Exploration Recording Sheet
*Order of Operations*

Many calculators are programmed to compute in a certain order, called the *order of operations.*

1. Determine the order the calculator follows for each expression in the window.

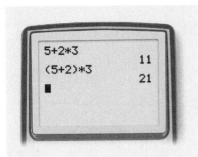

```
5+2*3
              11
(5+2)*3
              21
■
```

_____

_____

_____

_____

_____

**Use the necessary operation symbols +, −, ×, and ÷ and the grouping symbols ) and ( to make each statement true. Verify with your calculator.**

**2.** 4   3   6 = 7 _____      **3.** 4   3   6 = 6 _____

**4.** 4   3   6 = 22 _____      **5.** 4   3   6 = 42 _____

**6.** 4   3   6 = 2 _____      **7.** 6   3   4 = 8 _____

## Think and Discuss

8. **Explain** how the grouping symbols ) and ( are used in the order of operations.

_____

_____

9. **Describe** the order of operations in your own words.

_____

_____

_____

Holt Middle School Math   Course 2

Name _____ Date _____ Class _____

## Practice A
*Order of Operations*

**Choose the letter for the best answer.**

**1.** $75 + 12 \cdot 2$

   **A** 87           **C** 108

   **B** 99           **D** 174

**2.** $100 - 25 \div 5$

   **F** 15           **H** 80

   **G** 75          **J** 95

**3.** $50 - 18 \div 6 + 2$

   **A** 49           **C** 10

   **B** 40           **D** 4

**4.** $72 - 4^2 \cdot 2$

   **F** 32           **H** 56

   **G** 40          **J** 64

**5.** $(8 + 22) \div 5 + 5$

   **A** 30           **C** 11

   **B** 17.4        **D** 3

**6.** $3^3 - (9 \cdot 2 + 1)$

   **F** 19           **H** 8

   **G** 10          **J** −10

**Evaluate.**

**7.** $2^4 \div 8 + 5$

**8.** $18 + 2(1 + 3^2)$

**9.** $(16 \div 4) + 4 \cdot (2^2 - 2)$

**10.** $2^3 - (3 \cdot 5 - 8)$

**11.** $35 + 4^2 - (6 - 3)$

**12.** $6 \cdot 7 - 3(4 + 1)$

**13.** $100 \div 5 \cdot 2^2$

**14.** $(5 + 2)^2 \div 7 - 6$

**15.** $15 - 3 \cdot 4 \div 2 + 5$

**16.** Leon rents a video game for $5. He returns the video game 3 days late. The late fee is $1 for each day late. Evaluate the expression $5 + 3 \cdot 1$ to find out how much it costs Leon to rent the video game.

_____

**17.** Olivia shovels snow for 6 neighbors. Each neighbor pays her $8. Two neighbors each give her a $2 tip as well. Evaluate $6 \cdot 8 + 2 \cdot 2$ to find out how much money Olivia earns in all.

_____

**Holt Middle School Math**   **Course 2**

Name _____ Date _____ Class _____

# Practice B
## *Order of Operations*

**Evaluate.**

**1.** $15 \cdot 3 + 12 \cdot 2$

**2.** $212 + 21 \div 3$

**3.** $9 \cdot 3 - 18 \div 3$

_____

_____

_____

**4.** $65 - 36 \div 3$

**5.** $100 - 9^2 + 2$

**6.** $3 \cdot 5 - 45 \div 3^2$

_____

_____

_____

**7.** $54 \div 6 + 4 \cdot 6$

**8.** $(6 + 5) \cdot 16 \div 2$

**9.** $60 - 8 \cdot 12 \div 3$

_____

_____

_____

**10.** $45 - 3^2 \cdot 5$

**11.** $52 - (8 \cdot 2 \div 4) + 3^2$

**12.** $(2^3 + 10 \div 2) \cdot 3$

_____

_____

_____

**13.** $25 + 7(18 - 4^2)$

**14.** $(6 \cdot 3 - 12)^2 \div 9 + 7$

**15.** $4^3 - (3 + 12 \cdot 2 - 9)$

_____

_____

_____

**16.** $2^4 \div 8 + 5$

**17.** $(1 + 2)^2 \cdot (3 - 1)^2 \div 2$

**18.** $(16 \div 4) + 4 \cdot (2^2 - 2)$

_____

_____

_____

**19.** $2^5 - (3 \cdot 7 - 7)$

**20.** $75 + 5^2 - (8 - 3)$

**21.** $9 \cdot 6 - 5(10 - 3)$

_____

_____

_____

**22.** $96 \div 4 + 5 \cdot 2^2$

**23.** $(15 - 6)^2 \div 3 - 3^3$

**24.** $19 - 8 \cdot 5 \div 10 + 6 \div 3$

_____

_____

_____

**25.** Jared has $32. He buys 5 packs of trading cards that cost
$3 each and a display book that costs $7. Evaluate
$32 - (5 \cdot 3 + 7)$ to find out how much money Jared has left.

_____

**26.** David buys 3 movie tickets for $6 each and 2 bags of popcorn
for $2 each. Evaluate $3 \cdot 6 + 2 \cdot 2$ to find out how much money
David spent in all.

_____

Holt Middle School Math   Course 2

Name _____ Date _____ Class _____

**Evaluate.**

**1.** $25 \cdot 3 + 60 \cdot 2$

_____

**2.** $350 \div 5 + 12 \cdot 7$

_____

**3.** $3 \cdot 9 + 96 \div 4$

_____

**4.** $77 - 42 \div 7^1$

_____

**5.** $532 - 2^5 \div 4$

_____

**6.** $3(20 - 4^2) + 7$

_____

**7.** $270 \div 6 + 6^2$

_____

**8.** $(5 + 6)^2 + 18 \div 2$

_____

**9.** $10^2 - 25 \cdot 3 \div 5$

_____

**10.** $65 - 4^3 \cdot 1^7$

_____

**11.** $40 - (5 \cdot 2) + 8$

_____

**12.** $(6^2 + 4) \div 5$

_____

**13.** $2^4 \div 8 + 5$

_____

**14.** $(1 + 2)^2 \cdot (3 - 1)^2 \div 2$

_____

**15.** $(16 \div 4) + 4 \cdot (2^2 - 2)$

_____

**Insert grouping symbols to make a true statement.**

**16.** $18 + 2 \cdot 1 + 3^2 = 38$

_____

**17.** $4 \cdot 2 - 2^2 \div 9 + 2 = 6$

_____

**18.** $3^3 - 9 \cdot 2 + 1 = 8$

_____

**19.** $2^3 - 3 \cdot 5 - 8 = 1$

_____

**20.** $35 + 4^2 - 6 - 3 = 48$

_____

**21.** $6 \cdot 7 - 3 \cdot 4 + 1 = 27$

_____

**22.** A group of students charges $7 to clean the exterior and $6 to clean the interior of a car. They clean 9 exteriors and 5 interiors. Evaluate $7 \cdot 9 + 6 \cdot 5$ to find out how much money the students raised in all.

_____

**23.** Ariel has $65. She buys 5 books that cost $8.00 each, a bookmark that costs $2.00, and a magazine that costs $4.00. Evaluate $65 - (5 \cdot 8 + 2 + 4)$ to find out how much money Ariel has left.

_____

Holt Middle School Math   Course 2

Name _____ Date _____ Class _____

# Reteach
*Order of Operations*

To help you remember the order of operations use the phrase
"**P**lease **E**xcuse **M**y **D**ear **A**unt **S**ally."

---

**P**: first, **p**arentheses (if any)
**E**: second, **e**xponents (if any)
**M** and **D**: then, **m**ultiplication and **d**ivision, in order from left to right
**A** and **S**: finally, **a**ddition and **s**ubtraction, in order from left to right

---

Evaluate.                                              $39 \div (9 + 4) + 5 - 2^2$

Parentheses ⟶ $39 \div 13 + 5 - 2^2$

Exponents ⟶ $39 \div 13 + 5 - 4$

Multiply and divide from left to right ⟶ $3 + 5 - 4$

Add and subtract from left to right ⟶ $8 - 4 = 4$

**Evaluate.**

**1.** $12 \cdot 4 - 2$

_____ $- 2$

_____

**2.** $15 \div 3 \cdot 5$

_____ $\cdot 5$

_____

**3.** $15 \cdot 3 \div 5$

_____ $\div 5$

_____

**4.** $8 + 20 \div 4$

_____

**5.** $5 - 2 \cdot 6 \div 4 + 1$

_____

**6.** $3^2 + 6 \cdot 4 - 5^2$

_____

**7.** $1 + 4 \cdot 9 \div 6 - 7$

_____

**8.** $18 \div (6 \div 3)$

_____

**9.** $(18 \div 6) \div 3$

_____

**10.** $4 \cdot 5 + 8 \div 2 - 7$

_____

**11.** $2 \cdot 3 - 8 \div 2^2$

_____

**12.** $8(7 - 6) \div 2^3$

_____

**Holt Middle School Math   Course 2**

Name _____ Date _____ Class _____

# Challenge
## *Fixed and Variable Costs*

A *fixed cost* is a one-time cost. A *variable cost* changes depending on your use of a product or a service.

The annual enrollment fee per year at a fitness club (fixed cost) is $30. You also pay $2 per visit (variable cost), and you visit the club 8 times per month. What is your total annual cost?

$2 \cdot (8 \cdot 12)$      variable cost times total visits

$30 + 2 \cdot (8 \cdot 12)$      total annual cost

222      Your total annual cost is $222.

**Use the information above to solve problems 1–4.**

**1.** Suppose the annual fee is $25, but the cost per visit is $3. What is your annual cost?

**2.** Suppose you visit the club 3 times per week instead of 8 times per month. What is your annual cost?

**3.** Suppose the cost per visit is $3 after the first 50 visits per year. What is your annual cost?

**4.** Suppose you pay for up to 75 visits per year. Any additional visits are free. What is your annual cost?

The school band is raising money for a trip. The members ordered 5 dozen jerseys for $7 each and sold them for $12 each. They also ordered 4 dozen sweatshirts for $11 each and sold them for $18 each. The band paid $35 to create the design.

**5.** Write and evaluate an expression to calculate the band's variable costs for the clothing.

**6.** Write and evaluate an expression to calculate the band's total cost, including fixed costs.

**7.** Write and evaluate an expression to calculate the band's profit.

**8.** What would the profit be if jerseys sold for $10 and sweatshirts for $20?

Holt Middle School Math    **Course 2**

| LESSON | **Problem Solving** |
|--------|---------------------|
| **2-3** | *Order of Operations* |

## Write the correct answer.

**1.** In 1975, the minimum wage was $2.10 per hour. Write and evaluate an expression to show wages earned in a 35-hour week after a $12 tax deduction.

**2.** George bought 3 boxes of Girl Scout cookies at $3.50 per box and 4 boxes at $3.00 per box. Write and evaluate an expression to show his total cost.

**3.** In 1 week Ed works 4 days, 3 hours a day, for $12 per hour, and 2 days, 6 hours a day, for $15 per hour. Evaluate 12(4 • 3) + 15(2 • 6) to find Ed's weekly earnings.

**4.** Keisha had $150. She bought jeans for $27, a sweater for $32, 3 blouses for $16 each, and 2 pairs of socks for $6 each. Evaluate 150 − [27 + 32 + (3 • 16) + (2 • 6)] to find out how much money she has left.

## Choose the letter for the best answer.

**5.** As of September 1, 1997, the minimum wage was $5.15 per hour. How much more would someone earn now than in 1997 if she earns $5 more per hour for a 40-hour week?

**A** $206 more

**B** $200 more

**C** $406 more

**D** $400 more

**6.** Gary received $200 in birthday gifts. He bought 5 CDs for $15 each, 2 posters for $12 each, and a $70 jacket. How much money does he have left?

**F** $31

**G** $10

**H** $132

**J** $169

**7.** Yvonne took her younger brother and his friends to the movies. She bought 5 tickets for $8 each, 4 drinks for $2 each, and two $3 containers of popcorn. How much did she spend?

**A** $22

**B** $51

**C** $54

**D** $38

**8.** On a business trip, Mr. Chang stayed in a hotel for 7 nights. He paid $149 per night. While he was there, he made 8 phone calls at $2 each and charged $81 to room service. How much did he spend?

**F** $246

**G** $946

**H** $1,043

**J** $1,140

Holt Middle School Math   Course 2

## Puzzles, Twisters & Teasers

**LESSON 2-3** *Is Everything in Order?*

*What's the last thing you take off before you go to bed?*

**Decide whether each statement below is true or false. Use your answers to solve the riddle.**

1. A numerical expression is made up of numbers and operations.

   **T**          **F**

2. In mathematics, as in life, tasks may be done in any order.

   **T**          **F**

3. When using the order of operations, you should do division after subtraction.

   **T**          **F**

4. When using the order of operations, you should subtract and add from left to right.

   **T**          **F**

5. When using the order of operations, you should divide and multiply from right to left.

   **T**          **F**

6. When an expression has a set of grouping symbols within a second set of grouping symbols, you should begin with the innermost set.

   **T**          **F**

7. You should perform operations inside parentheses first.

   **T**          **F**

8. When using the order of operations, you should evaluate the exponent expression after multiplying and adding.

   **T**          **F**

9. Mathematicians agree on using the order of operations.

   **T**          **F**

| **T** |
|---|
| L F Y |
| R H |

| **F** |
|---|
| O T |
| E U |

You take ____  ____  ____  ____    ____  ____  ____  ____    ____  ____  ____
        T     F     F     T      T     F     F     F      F     T     T

____  ____  ____  ____  ____  ____  ____  ____.
  F     T     F     T     T     F     F     T

| Lesson | Materials | Resources |
|---|---|---|
| Hands-On Lab 2B<br>Divisibility<br>  NCTM: Number and Operations<br>  Understand numbers (See p. T00.)<br>  • Use factors. | **Required**<br>100 Chart *Hands-On Lab Activities* | • *Hands-On Lab Activities*, pp. 00-00 |
| Lesson 2-4<br>Prime Factorization<br>  NCTM: Number and Operations<br>  Understand numbers (See p. T00.)<br>  • Use prime factorization. | **Optional**<br>Grid paper, p. 000 CRB | • *Chapter 2 Resource Book*, pp. 00–00<br>• Daily Transparency, TXX CRB<br>• Additional Examples Transparency, TXX CRB<br>• *Alternate Openers: Explorations*, p. 13 |
| Lesson 2-5<br>Greatest Common Factor<br>  NCTM: Number and Operations<br>  Understand numbers (See p. T00.)<br>  • Use factors | **Optional**<br>Two-color counters MK | • *Chapter 2 Resource Book*, pp. 00–00<br>• Daily Transparency, TXX CRB<br>• Additional Examples Transparency, TXX CRB<br>• *Alternate Openers: Explorations*, p. 14 |
| Lesson 2-6<br>Least Common Multiple<br>  NCTM: Number and Operations<br>  Understand numbers (See p. T00.)<br>  • Use multiples. | **Optional**<br>Calendar for September<br>Calculators, p. 000 CRB | • *Chapter 2 Resource Book*, pp. 00–00<br>• Daily Transparency, TXX CRB<br>• Additional Examples Transparency, TXX CRB<br>• *Alternate Openers: Explorations*, p. 15 |
| Section 2B<br>Assessment | | • Mid-Chapter Quiz, SE p. 90<br>• Section 2B Quiz, AR p. 9<br>• *Test and Practice Generator* CD-ROM |

**SE** = Student Edition   **TE** = Teacher's Edition   **AR** = Assessment Resources
**CRB** = Chapter Resource Book   **MK** = Manipulatives Kit

## 2-7 Variables and Algebraic Expressions

Suzanne entered a walk-a-thon for a local charity. Her sponsor provided the $20 entry fee and will provide $4 for each mile she walks.

**1.** Complete the table.

| Miles Walked | Expression | Amount ($) |
|:---:|:---:|:---:|
| 1 | 20 + 4(1) | 24 |
| 2 | 20 + 4(2) | |
| 3 | | |
| 4 | | |
| 5 | | |
| 6 | | |

**2.** If Suzanne walks 12 miles, how much money will she collect for the charity?

**3.** Suppose Suzanne wants to give $100 to the charity. How many miles must she walk?

## Think and Discuss

**4. Explain** how the number of miles walked is used to determine the amount of money collected.

**5. Describe** how to write an expression for the amount of money collected if the number of miles walked is replaced by the variable $m$.

**This page is available as a transparency.**

Holt Middle School Math  Course 2

# Exploration Recording Sheet

**LESSON 2-7**

## *Variables and Algebraic Expressions*

Suzanne entered a walk-a-thon for a local charity. Her sponsor provided the $20 entry fee and will provide $4 for each mile she walks.

**1.** Complete the table.

| Miles Walked | Expression | Amount (s) |
|---|---|---|
| 1 | 20 + 4(1) | 24 |
| 2 | 20 + 4(2) | |
| 3 | | |
| 4 | | |
| 5 | | |
| 6 | | |

**2.** If Suzanne walks 12 miles, how much money will she collect for the charity?

_____

**3.** Suppose Suzanne wants to give $100 to the charity. How many miles must she walk?

_____

## Think and Discuss

**4. Explain** how the number of miles walked is used to determine the amount of money collected.

_____

_____

**5. Describe** how to write an expression for the amount of money collected if the number of miles walked is replaced by the variable *m*.

_____

_____

Holt Middle School Math   Course 2

Name _____ Date _____ Class _____

# Variables and Algebraic Expressions

**Find the value of $n + 3$ for each value of $n$.**

**1.** $n = 4$        **2.** $n = 7$        **3.** $n = 0$        **4.** $n = 32$

_____     _____     _____     _____

**Find the value of $x - 9$ for each value of $x$.**

**5.** $x = 12$        **6.** $x = 57$        **7.** $x = 19$        **8.** $x = 100$

_____     _____     _____     _____

**Find the value of each expression using the given value for each variable.**

**9.** $3n$ for $n = 4$        **10.** $x + 8$ for $x = 8$        **11.** $9p - 6$ for $p = 2$

_____     _____     _____

**12.** $n \div 5$ for $n = 35$        **13.** $6x + 18$ for $x = 0$        **14.** $s - 7$ for $s = 8$

_____     _____     _____

**15.** $3w + 5$ for $w = 3$        **16.** $c - 9$ for $c = 12$        **17.** $2a \div 3$ for $a = 6$

_____     _____     _____

**18.** $y + z$ for $y = 10$ and $z = 20$        **19.** $3w - 2v$ for $w = 7$ and $v = 8$

_____          _____

**20.** $4a \div b$ for $a = 6$ and $b = 4$        **21.** $5s + 4t$ for $s = 3$ and $t = 4$

_____          _____

**22.** The expression $7w$ gives the number of days in $w$ weeks. Find the value of $7w$ for $w = 20$. How many days are there in 20 weeks? _____

**23.** A cat can run as fast as $m \div 2$ miles per minute in $m$ minutes. Find the value of $m \div 2$ for $m = 10$. How many miles can a cat run in 10 minutes? _____

**24.** Tyrone works 8 hours a day. You can use the expression $8d$ to find the total number of hours he works in $d$ days. How many hours does he work in 5 days? _____

Holt Middle School Math   Course 2

## LESSON 2-7 **Practice B**

### *Variables and Algebraic Expressions*

**Evaluate $n - 5$ for each value of $n$.**

**1.** $n = 8$  **2.** $n = 121$  **3.** $n = 32$  **4.** $n = 59$

_____  _____  _____  _____

**Evaluate each algebraic expression for the given variable values.**

**5.** $3n + 15$ for $n = 4$  **6.** $h \div 12$ for $h = 60$  **7.** $32x - 32$ for $x = 2$

_____  _____  _____

**8.** $\frac{c}{2}$ for $c = 24$  **9.** $(n \div 2)5$ for $n = 14$  **10.** $8p + 148$ for $p = 15$

_____  _____  _____

**11.** $e^2 - 7$ for $e = 8$  **12.** $3d^2 + d$ for $d = 5$  **13.** $40 - 4k^3$ for $k = 2$

_____  _____  _____

**14.** $2y - z$ for $y = 21$ and $z = 19$  **15.** $3h^2 + 8m$ for $h = 3$ and $m = 2$

_____  _____

**16.** $18 \div a + b \div 9$ for $a = 6$ and $b = 45$  **17.** $10x - 4y$ for $x = 14$ and $y = 5$

_____  _____

**18.** You can find the area of a rectangle with the expression $lw$ where $l$ represents the length and $w$ represents the width. What is the area of the rectangle at right in square feet?

5 ft

2 ft

_____

**19.** Rita drove an average of 55 mi/h on her trip to the mountains. You can use the expression $55h$ to find out how many miles she drove in $h$ hours. If she drove for 5 hours, how many miles did she drive?

_____

Holt Middle School Math   Course 2

Name _____ Date _____ Class _____

**Evaluate each algebraic expression for the given variable values.**

**1.** $3n + 4n$ for $n = 8$

_____

**2.** $\dfrac{6s}{5}$ for $s = 25$

_____

**3.** $q^2 + 5q - 11$ for $q = 4$

_____

**4.** $\dfrac{350}{d} + 4d + 7$ for $d = 10$

_____

**5.** $9x + 2x^2 + 2$ for $x = 2$

_____

**6.** $8m^2 + 7 - 2m$ for $m = 3$

_____

**7.** $4(h + k)$ for $h = 3$ and $k = 55$

_____

**8.** $\dfrac{6r}{4} + 5s$ for $r = 8$ and $s = 18$

_____

**9.** $6a - 2b^2$ for $a = 9$ and $b = 5$

_____

**10.** $6h - 20g$ for $h = 1{,}500$ and $g = 200$

_____

**11.** $\dfrac{36}{m^2} + \dfrac{n^2}{4}$ for $m = 6$ and $n = 16$

_____

**12.** $x^2 - 2x - y^2$ for $x = 15$ and $y = 2$

_____

**13.** $4d^3 + 6e^2 - \dfrac{8d}{2}$ for $d = 2$ and $e = 3$

_____

**14.** $\dfrac{5r^2}{4} + \dfrac{4s}{3r}$ for $r = 4$ and $s = 9$

_____

**15.** You can find the volume of a rectangular prism with the expression $a \bullet b \bullet c$, where $a$ is the length, $b$ is the width, and $c$ is the height of the prism. What is the volume of the prism at right in cubic inches?

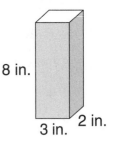

8 in.

3 in.  2 in.

_____

**16.** You can use the expression $5m$ to find out how many seconds it takes a sound to travel $m$ miles through the air. However, through water, sound takes $m$ seconds to travel $m$ miles. Use the expression $5m - m$ to find out how much longer will it take a sound to travel 8 miles in air than in water.

_____

Holt Middle School Math   Course 2

**LESSON 2-7**

# Reteach
## *Variables and Algebraic Expressions*

A **variable** is a letter that represents a number than can change in an expression. When you **evaluate** an algebraic expression, you substitute the value given for the variable in the expression.

- Algebraic expression: $x - 3$

  The value of the expression depends on the value of the variable $x$.

  If $x = 7 \rightarrow 7 - 3 = 4$

  If $x = 11 \rightarrow 11 - 3 = 8$

  If $x = 15 \rightarrow 15 - 3 = 12$

- Evaluate $4n + 1$ for $n = 5$.

  Replace the variable $n$ with 5. $\rightarrow 4(5) + 1 = 20 + 1 = 21$

**Evaluate each expression for the given value.**

**1.** $a + 7$ for $a = 3$

   $a + 7 = 3 + 7 =$ _____

**2.** $k - 5$ for $k = 13$

   $k - 5 =$ _____ $- 5 =$ _____

**3.** $y \div 3$ for $y = 6$

   $y \div 3 =$ _____ $\div 3 =$ _____

**4.** $12 + m$ for $m = 9$

   $12 + m =$ _____ $+$ _____ $=$ _____

**5.** $3n - 2$ for $n = 5$

   $3n - 2 = 3($_____$) - 2 =$ _____ $- 2 =$ _____

**6.** $5x + 4$ for $x = 4$

   $5x + 4 = 5($_____$) +$ _____ $=$ _____ $+$ _____ $=$ _____

**7.** $c - 9$ for $c = 11$

_____

**8.** $b + 16$ for $b = 4$

_____

**9.** $a - 4$ for $a = 9$

_____

**10.** $25 - g$ for $g = 12$

_____

**11.** $w + 5$ for $w = 2$

_____

**12.** $3 + s$ for $s = 8$

_____

**13.** $7q$ for $q = 10$

_____

**14.** $2y + 9$ for $y = 8$

_____

**15.** $6x - 3$ for $x = 1$

_____

Holt Middle School Math   Course 2

Name _____ Date _____ Class _____

# Challenge
## *What an Expression!*

Complete each table with four expressions that have the same value. Use each given value of *n*.

**1.**

| Expression Value 32 | Value of *n* 4 |
|---|---|
| Addition expression: | |
| Subtraction expression: | |
| Multiplication expression: | |
| Division expression: | |

**2.**

| Expression Value 96 | Value of *n* 12 |
|---|---|
| Addition expression: | |
| Subtraction expression: | |
| Multiplication expression: | |
| Division expression: | |

**3.**

| Expression Value 156 | Value of *n* 6 |
|---|---|
| Addition expression: | |
| Subtraction expression: | |
| Multiplication expression: | |
| Division expression: | |

**4.**

| Expression Value 98 | Value of *n* 14 |
|---|---|
| Addition expression: | |
| Subtraction expression: | |
| Multiplication expression: | |
| Division expression: | |

**5.**

| Expression Value 57 | Value of *n* 12 |
|---|---|
| Addition expression: | |
| Subtraction expression: | |
| Multiplication expression: | |
| Division expression: | |

**6.**

| Expression Value 248 | Value of *n* 124 |
|---|---|
| Addition expression: | |
| Subtraction expression: | |
| Multiplication expression: | |
| Division expression: | |

Holt Middle School Math   Course 2

Name _____ Date _____ Class _____

# Problem Solving
## *Variables and Expressions*

**Write the correct answer.**

1. In 2000, people in the United States watched television an average of 29 hours per week. Use the expression 29*w* for *w* = 4 to find out about how many hours per month this is.

   _____

2. Find the value of the variable *w* in the expression 29*w* to find the average number of hours people watched television in a year. Find the value of the expression.

   _____

3. The expression *y* + 45 gives the year when a person will be 45 years old, where *y* is the year of birth. When will a person born in 1992 be 45 years old?

   _____

4. The expression 24*g* gives the number of miles Guy's car can travel on *g* gallons of gas. If the car has 6 gallons of gas left, how much farther can he drive?

   _____

**Choose the letter for the best answer.**

5. Sam is 5 feet tall. The expression 0.5*m* + 60 can be used to calculate his height in inches if he grows an average of 0.5 inch each month. How tall will Sam be in 6 months?

   A 56 inches

   B 5 feet 6 inches

   C 63 inches

   D 53 inches

6. The winner of the 1911 Indianapolis 500 auto race drove at a speed of about *s* − 56 mi/h, where *s* is the 2001 winning speed of about 131 mi/h. What was the approximate winning speed in 1911?

   F 75 mi/h

   G 186 mi/h

   H 85 mi/h

   J 187 mi/h

7. The expression 1,587*v* gives the number of pounds of waste produced per person in the United States in *v* years. How many pounds of waste per person is produced in the United States in 6 years?

   A 1,581 pounds

   B 1,593 pounds

   C 9,348 pounds

   D 9,522 pounds

8. The expression $1.25*p* + $3.50 can be used to calculate the total charge for faxing *p* pages at a business services store. How much would it cost to fax 8 pages?

   F $12.50

   G $4.75

   H $13.50

   J $10.00

Holt Middle School Math   Course 2

# Puzzles, Twisters & Teasers
## *Movie Math!*

Circle words from the list in the word search. Then find an extra
word in the word search that best completes the riddle.

expression    substitute    variable    value

constant    evaluate    algebra    algebraic

```
V A L U E S D E X P R E S S I O N
Q A C V B N M V A S D F U B H U I
W L R L K J G A C T U P B V M A L
E G G I L S P L A S H W S I K L V
R E C V A R T U M J U I T C V G N
T B N H T B O A S D F G I P O E U
Y R X O P N L T E R W T T Y T B E
U A V G T M K E U H B J U W Q R D
O I P O I U Y T F I J O T A X A G
P C O N S T A N T D F G E Z X C V
```

This Ron Howard movie was all wet.

_____  _____  _____  _____  _____  _____

Holt Middle School Math    Course 2

# EXPLORATION

## 2-8 Translate Words into Math

Follow the steps below, showing your work for each step.

**Step 1:** Choose any whole number between 1 and 10.

**Step 2:** Add to it the next two whole numbers that come after it.

**Step 3:** Divide the result by 3.

**Step 4:** Subtract the number that you began with.

**Step 5:** Tell what number you end with.

1. Compare your results with any other students who began with the same whole number for Step 1. Do your results agree?

2. Compare your results with any other students who did not begin with the same whole number for Step 1. Do your results agree?

## Think and Discuss

3. **Describe** the operation in step 2. What numbers are involved?
4. **Look for a pattern** in all the results. Describe what you find.

**This page is available as a transparency.**

Name _____ Date _____ Class _____

# Exploration Recording Sheet
*Translate Words into Math*

**Follow the steps below, showing your work for each step.**

**Step 1:** Choose any whole number between 1 and 10.

**Step 2:** Add to it the next two whole numbers that come after it.

**Step 3:** Divide the result by 3.

**Step 4:** Subtract the number that you began with.

**Step 5:** Tell what number you end with.

1. Compare your results with any other students who began with the same whole number for Step 1. Do your results agree?

_____

_____

2. Compare your results with any other students who did not begin with the same whole number for Step 1. Do your results agree?

_____

_____

## Think and Discuss

3. **Describe** the operation in step 2. What numbers are involved?

_____

_____

4. **Look for a pattern** in all the results. Describe what you find.

_____

_____

Holt Middle School Math   Course 2

## LESSON 2-8 **Practice A**
### *Translate Words Into Math*

**Write as an algebraic expression.**

**1.** the sum of $m$ and 8

_____

**2.** the product of 3 and $n$

_____

**3.** 4 less than $x$

_____

**4.** the quotient of a number and 12

_____

**5.** 52 times a number

_____

**6.** $w$ less than 15

_____

**7.** the sum of 13 and a number

_____

**8.** the sum of 5 times $p$ and 10

_____

**9.** the sum of 15 divided by $b$ and 6

_____

**10.** 12 less than the amount $y$ divided by 2

_____

**11.** 26 increased by 12 times a number _____

**12.** the difference of 2 times a number and 6 _____

**13.** the product of $h$ and 3, increased by 20 _____

**14.** 18 less than the product of a number and 4 _____

**15.** take away 32 from the product of 6 and a number _____

**16.** Used video games cost $25 each. Write an expression to
find the cost of $m$ video games.                           _____

**17.** Sal earned $740 for $n$ weeks of work. Write an expression
for the amount he earned each week.                        _____

**18.** As of the 2000–2001 NBA season, Reggie Miller is the
all-time leader in 3-point field goals made. He made $n$
more field goals than Dale Ellis. Dale Ellis made 1,719
3-pointers. Write an expression to find the number of
3-pointers Reggie Miller made.                             _____

**19.** The $2 bill has Thomas Jefferson on the front of it.
Write an expression to find out how much money $v$ bills
with Thomas Jefferson on them would be worth.              _____

**Holt Middle School Math   Course 2**

Name _____ Date _____ Class _____

**Write as an algebraic expression.**

**1.** 125 decreased by a number

_____

**2.** 359 more than *z*

_____

**3.** the product of a number and 35

_____

**4.** the quotient of 100 and *w*

_____

**5.** twice a number, plus 27

_____

**6.** 12 less than 15 times *x*

_____

**7.** the product of *e* and 4, divided by 12

_____

**8.** *y* less than 18 times 6

_____

**9.** 48 more than the quotient of a number and 64 _____

**10.** 500 less than the product of 4 and a number _____

**11.** the quotient of *p* and 4, decreased by 320 _____

**12.** 13 multiplied by the amount 60 minus *w* _____

**13.** the quotient of 45 and the sum of *c* and 17 _____

**14.** twice the sum of a number and 600 _____

**15.** There are twice as many flute players as there are trumpet players in the band. If there are *n* flute players, write an expression to find out how many trumpet players there are. _____

**16.** The Nile River is the longest river in the world at 4,160 miles. A group of explorers traveled along the entire Nile in *x* days. They traveled the same distance each day. Write an expression to find each day's distance. _____

**17.** A slice of pizza has 290 calories, and a stalk of celery has 5 calories. Write an expression to find out how many calories there are in *a* slices of pizza and *b* stalks of celery. _____

**18.** Grant pays 10¢ per minute plus $5 per month for telephone long distance. Write an expression for *m* minutes of long-distance calls in one month. _____

Holt Middle School Math   Course 2

## LESSON 2-8 Practice C
### *Translate Words Into Math*

**Write as an algebraic expression.**

1. the product of 6 and the square of a number _____

2. the square of the product of 6 and a number _____

3. 4 times the sum of a number and 6,008 _____

4. 200 less than half of a number _____

5. 3 times the difference of a number squared and 82 _____

6. 999 less than 45 increased by the product of a number

    and 85 _____

**Write a verbal expression for each algebraic expression.**

7. $2(4n)$ _____

8. $100 - \dfrac{54}{w}$ _____

9. $r^2 + 4r + 7$ _____

10. $\dfrac{45}{5s^2}$ _____

11. An albatross can sleep while flying 25 mi/h. An albatross flew 3 miles awake and another $n$ hours asleep at 25 mi/h. Write an expression to find the distance flown. _____

12. You have $d$ dimes, $q$ quarters, and $n$ nickels. Write an expression to find the total amount of money. _____

13. Four out of every 10 homes in the United States have a dog. Write an expression to find out how many dogs there are in $h$ homes. _____

14. A waitress who worked $k$ hours earned $32 in tips. She gets an additional salary of $4.50 per hour. Write an expression to find the amount she earned. _____

Holt Middle School Math   Course 2

# Reteach

## 2-8 Translate Words Into Math

Use the operation clues in a word phrase to translate word phrases into algebraic expressions.

| Addition | |
|---|---|
| add | plus |
| sum | more than |
| increased by | |

| Subtraction | |
|---|---|
| subtract | minus |
| difference | less than |
| decreased by | take away |

| Multiplication |
|---|
| times |
| multiplied by |
| product |

| Division |
|---|
| divided by |
| divided into |
| quotient |

**Write an algebraic expression for the difference of a number and 8.**

**1.** What operation would you choose? _____

**2.** Write an algebraic expression. _____

**Write an algebraic expression for 3 more than a number.**

**3.** What operation would you choose? _____

**4.** Write an algebraic expression. _____

**Write an algebraic expression for the quotient of a number and 15.**

**5.** What operation would you choose? _____

**6.** Write an algebraic expression. _____

**Write an algebraic expression.**

**7.** the product of 12 and a number $k$ _____

**8.** a number $d$ increased by 9 _____

**9.** a number $h$ divided by 4 _____

## Challenge

**LESSON 2-8**

### *What's My Equation?*

Match each equation with the word problem it represents. Write
the equation and corresponding letter. Then write the letter of
the equation in the circle that has the problem number.
Discover the message formed by the letters.

| | | | |
|---|---|---|---|
| **P** $2k = 14$ | **D** $\frac{p}{3} = 2.50$ | **A** $\frac{m}{5} = 8$ | **U** $3t = 21$ |
| **M** $a - 18 = 33$ | **S** $w + 7 = 25$ | **T** $x + 7 = 22$ | **H** $n - 12 = 37$ |

1. Tom has 7 more CDs than Rick does.
   If Tom has 22 CDs, how many does
   Rick have?                                        _____     2

2. Maria is 18 years younger than Kim.
   If Maria is 33, how old is Kim?                     _____     3

3. Five friends went out for dinner. They
   shared the cost of the meal equally. If
   each person paid $8, what was the
   total cost of the meal?                             _____     1

4. Max paid 3 times as much for a tape
   as his friend did. If Max paid $21, how
   much did his friend pay?                            _____     8

5. Marisa and her two friends share a
   pizza. The cost of the pizza is shared
   equally among them. If each person
   pays $2.50, how much does the
   pizza cost?                                         _____     3

6. Lee has scored twice as many goals
   as Jiang has. If Lee's goal total is 14,
   how many goals has Jiang scored?                    _____    5

7. Jamal sold 7 more magazine
   subscriptions than Wayne did. If Jamal
   sold 25 subscriptions, how many did
   Wayne sell?                                         _____     5

8. Shelly delivered 12 fewer newspapers
   this week than last week. If she
   delivered 37 papers this week, how
   many did she deliver last week?                     _____     7

 4

 6

Holt Middle School Math   Course 2

Name _____ Date _____ Class _____

## LESSON 2-8 Problem Solving

### Translate Words into Math

**Write the correct answer.**

1. Employers in the United States allocate $n$ fewer vacation days than the 25 days given by the average Japanese employer. Write an expression to show the number of vacation days given U.S. workers.

_____

2. There are 112 members in the Somerset Marching Band. They will march in $r$ equal rows. Write an expression for the number of band members in each row.

_____

3. A cup of cottage cheese has 26 grams of protein. Write an expression for the amount of protein in $s$ cups of cottage cheese.

_____

4. Every morning Sasha exercises for 20 minutes. She exercises $k$ minutes every evening. Next week she will double her exercise time at night. Write an expression to show how long Sasha will exercise each day next week.

_____

**Choose the letter for the best answer.**

5. One centimeter equals 0.3937 inches. Which expression shows how many inches are in $c$ centimeters?

   A  $0.3937 + c$

   B  $0.3937 \div c$

   C  $c \div 0.3937$

   D  $0.3937c$

6. In 1957, the Soviet Union launched *Sputnik 1,* the first satellite to orbit Earth. It circled Earth's orbit every 1.6 hours for 92 days, then burned up. If the satellite traveled $m$ miles per hour, which expression shows the length of the orbit?

   F  $92m$

   G  $1.6m$

   H  $m \div 1.6$

   J  $92 \div m$

7. Gina's heart rate is 70 beats per minute. Which expression shows the number of beats in $h$ hours?

   A  $70h$

   B  $60h$

   C  $4{,}200h$

   D  $3{,}600h$

8. The Harris family went on vacation for $w$ weeks and 3 days. Which expression shows the total number of days of their vacation?

   F  $7w$

   G  $3w$

   H  $7w + 3$

   J  $3w + 7$

Holt Middle School Math   Course 2

# Puzzles, Twisters & Teasers

**LESSON 2-8** *Birds of a Feather!*

Solve the crossword puzzle. Then use the letters in the shaded boxes to answer the riddle. You'll need to use some letters more than once.

**Across**

1. something that does not change
2. a number or symbol placed to the right of and above another number, symbol, or expression
6. putting together
8. the letter in a term
9. a number, a variable, or a product of numbers and variables

**Down**

1. the number in a term
3. the multiple expressed by an exponent
4. a symbol used for counting
5. group similar objects
7. similar

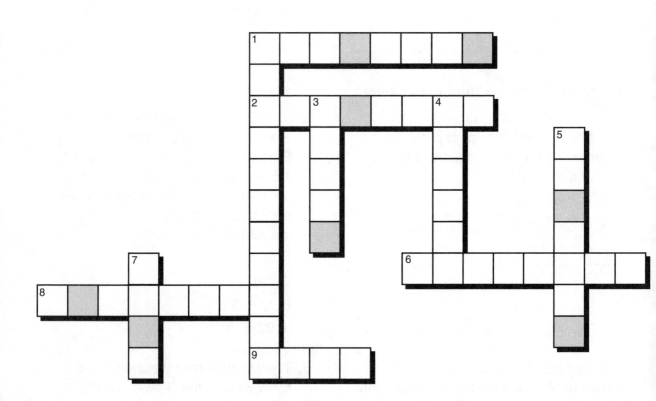

Where do birds invest their money?

In the ____ ____ ____ ____ ____ ____ ____ ____ ____ ____ ____.

Holt Middle School Math   Course 2

## 2-9 Combining Like Terms

Philipe is organizing the storerooms at an athletic club. He finds **3 cases** and **2 cans** of tennis balls in one room and **5 cases** and **6 cans** of tennis balls in another room. He combines them and has **8 cases** and **8 cans.**

You can represent this situation with algebra tiles and with symbols.

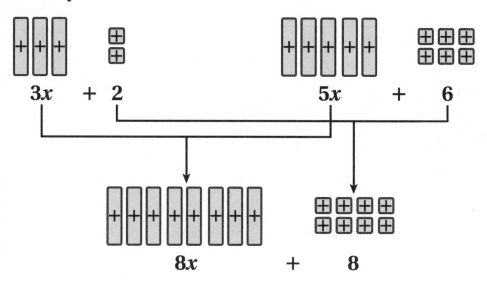

Draw algebra tiles to represent each expression, and combine like terms.

**1.** $4x + 6x$

**2.** $5x + 2 + 7x$

**3.** $x + 1 + 2x + 7$

**4.** $3x + 4 + 3x + 5$

## Think and Discuss

**5. Discuss** your method for combining like terms.

**6. Explain** what you could combine when adding $3x + 2 + 5x$.

**This page is available as a transparency.**

Holt Middle School Math   Course 2

## Exploration Recording Sheet

**LESSON 2-9** *Combining Like Terms*

Philipe is organizing the storerooms at an athletic club.
He finds **3 cases** and **2 cans** of tennis balls in one room
and **5 cases** and **6 cans** of tennis balls in another room.
He combines them and has **8 cases** and **8 cans**.

You can represent this situation with algebra tiles and
with symbols.

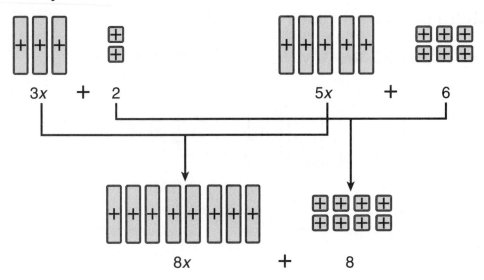

Draw algebra tiles to represent each expression, and combine
like terms.

**1.** $4x + 6x$

**2.** $5x + 2 + 7x$

Holt Middle School Math    Course 2

# Exploration Recording Sheet

## LESSON 2-9 Combining Like Terms (continued)

**3.** $x + 1 + 2x + 7$

**4.** $3x + 4 + 3x + 5$

## Think and Discuss

**5. Discuss** your method for combining like terms.

_____

_____

**6. Explain** what you could combine when adding
$3x + 2 + 5x$.

_____

_____

**Holt Middle School Math    Course 2**

## Practice A
**LESSON 2-9** *Combining Like Terms*

**Identify like terms.**

1. $6a$  $b$  $a$  $17$  $4b$  $32$  $17a$

_____

2. $x$  $x^2$  $3x$  $3$  $3x^2$  $6$

_____

3. $2$  $6z$  $6z^2$  $z$  $17z$  $z^2$  $3$

_____

4. $m$  $8$  $8m^2$  $8m$  $m^2$  $12m$  $18$

_____

5. $2p$  $22p$  $56q$  $12^2$  $q$  $34$

_____

6. $d$  $d^2$  $15d^2$  $2d$  $4^2$  $5d$  $44$

_____

**Combine like terms.**

7. $6p^2 + 3p^2$

_____

8. $9x - 6x$

_____

9. $a^2 + b^2 + 2a^2 + 5b^2$

_____

10. $7h^2 + 3 - 2h^2 + 4$

_____

11. $3x + 3y + x + y + z$

_____

12. $5b + 5b + 6b^2 - 10 - 3b$

_____

13. Find the perimeter of the rectangle. Combine like terms.

   **A** $4x + 3y$

   **B** $8x + 6y$

   **C** $12xy$

   **D** $4x^2 + 3y^2$

$4x$

$3y$

Holt Middle School Math   Course 2

Name _____ Date _____ Class _____

**Identify like terms.**

1. $3a$  $b^2$  $b^3$  $4b^2$  $4$  $5a$

_____

2. $x$  $x^4$  $4x$  $4x^2$  $4x^4$  $3x^2$

_____

3. $6m$  $6m^2$  $n^2$  $2n$  $2$  $4m$  $5n$

_____

4. $12s$  $7s^4$  $9s$  $s^2$  $5$  $5s^4$  $2$

_____

**Combine like terms.**

5. $2p + 22q^2 - p$              6. $x^2 + 3x^2 - 4^2$

_____   _____

7. $n^4 + n^3 + 3n - n - n^3$    8. $4a + 4b + 2 - 2a + 5b - 1$

_____   _____

9. $32m^2 + 14n^2 - 12m^2 + 5n - 3$   10. $2h^2 + 3g - 2h^2 + 2^2 - 3 + 4g$

_____   _____

11. Write an expression for the perimeter of the figure at right. Combine like terms in the expression.

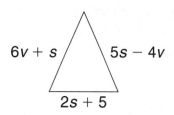

_____

12. Write an expression for the combined perimeters of the figures at right. Combine like terms in the expression.

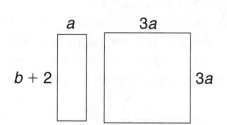

_____

Holt Middle School Math   Course 2

Name _____ Date _____ Class _____

**Combine like terms.**

1. $8k^2 + 4k - 3k^2 + 3^2 - k + 5$

   _____

2. $10x^3 + 5y^2 + 2xy - 4y^2 + 4xy - x^3$

   _____

3. $3a + 2b^2 + 6c + a - 2c + b^2 + c$

   _____

4. $12x^4 + 6x^2 + 5x^3 - x^2 + 2xy - 8x^4$

   _____

5. $9p^6 + q^2 + 6p + 5q^2 + 5p - 5q^2$

   _____

6. $h^2 + 4h + 4h^2 - h + 4 + h^2 + 7h$

   _____

7. Write an expression that has five terms and simplifies to
   $5m^3 + 4n$ when you combine like terms.

   _____

8. Write an expression for the perimeter
   of the figure to the right. Combine like
   terms in the expression.

   _____

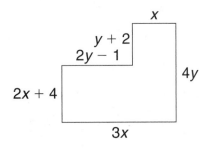

9. Write an expression to find the
   combined perimeters of the figures to
   the right. Combine like terms in the
   expression.

   _____

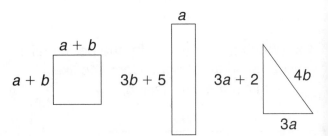

10. Jake scored *x* points in the first basketball game. He scored
    2 fewer points in the next game. His teammate, Jack, scored
    2*y* points in the first game and 4 more than twice as many points
    in the next game. Write an expression for the total number of
    points scored by both players and combine like terms.

    _____

**Holt Middle School Math  Course 2**

Name _____ Date _____ Class _____

# Reteach
## Combining Like Terms

Look at the following expressions: $x = 1x$

$x + x = 2x$

$x + x + x = 3x$

The numbers 1, 2, and 3 are called **coefficients** of $x$.

**Identify each coefficient.**

**1.** $3n$ _____    **2.** $7y$ _____    **3.** $m$ _____    **4.** $9$ _____

An algebraic expression has terms that are separated by + and −.
In the expression $2x + 5y$, the **terms** are $2x$ and $5y$.

| Expression | Terms |
|:---:|:---:|
| $8x + 4y$ | $8x$ and $4y$ |
| $m - 3n$ | $m$ and $3n$ |
| $4a^2 - 2b + a$ | $4a^2$, $2b$, and $a$ |
| $6d \div 2p$ | $6d$ and $2p$ |

Sometimes the terms of an expression can be combined.
Only **like terms** can be combined.

$7w + w$        like terms

$2x - 2y + 2$    unlike terms because $x$ and $y$ are different variables

$8e - 3e + 2e$  like terms

$5d + 25g$      unlike terms because $d$ and $g$ are different variables

To simplify an expression:
**Step 1:** Combine like terms.
**Step 2:** Add or subtract the coefficients of the variable.

$7w + w = 8w$

$6y + 1 - 3y = 3y + 1$

**Combine like terms.**

**5.** $y + 5y$          **6.** $9x - 4x$          **7.** $5s - 2s$          **8.** $3d + 7d$

_____          _____          _____          _____

**9.** $3b + b + 6$      **10.** $8a - a - 3$      **11.** $2p + 4p + r$      **12.** $9b - 8b + c$

_____          _____          _____          _____

Holt Middle School Math   Course 2

Name _____ Date _____ Class _____

# Challenge
## *Matching Terms*

Draw a line from each set of terms in Column A to its equivalent combination in Column B. Then circle each letter in Column B that does not have a matching term. Unscramble those letters to answer the riddle.

| Column A | Column B |
|---|---|
| 1. $2x + 7 + 5x - 4 - x$ | A. $5y + 9x + 12$ |
| 2. $5 + 7x + 2x - 3 + 6$ | B. $12y + 6x + 24$ |
| 3. $x + y + 4x - 3x + 2y + 3y$ | C. $15$ |
| 4. $3x^2 + 5x - 17 + 6x + 20$ | D. $9x + 8$ |
| 5. $4x + x^2 + 12 - 4 + 2x$ | E. $4$ |
| 6. $12y + 12x + 12 - 6x + 12$ | F. $6x + 3$ |
| 7. $12y + 4 + x - 7y + 8 + 8x$ | G. $11x + y + 7$ |
| 8. $5x + x^2 + 2x + 5 - 4 - x^2$ | H. $x^2 + 6x + 8$ |
| 9. $5x^2 + 8x + 7x^2 + 6x$ | I. $4x$ |
| 10. $12x + 6 - 8x - 4x - 3 + 12$ | J. $3x^2 + 11x + 3$ |
| 11. $5x + 4 - 3x + 5 + 2x - 9$ | K. $3x + 2$ |
| 12. $4x + 2y + 8 - 3 - y - x$ | L. $3x^2$ |
| 13. $4x + 5 + 7x + 2y + 2 - y$ | M. $6x$ |
| 14. $2y + 2x + 8 - 6 + x - 2y$ | N. $x^2 + 3x$ |
| 15. $4x + 6y + 6 + 7x + y$ | O. $6x^2 + 6y + 1$ |
| 16. $3x^2 + 4x - 2x^2 - 3x + 2x$ | P. $12x^2 + 14x$ |
| 17. $8x + 4 - 4 - 4x + x$ | Q. $7x + 1$ |
| 18. $y + 5x + 6y + 9 - 6$ | R. $x^2$ |
| 19. $x^2 + 3 + 2x^2 + 4 - 7$ | S. $5x + 7y + 3$ |
| 20. $5y + 3 + 7x^2 - 2 - x^2 + y$ | T. $0$ |
| | U. $2x + 6y$ |
| | V. $3x + y + 5$ |
| | W. $11x + 7y + 6$ |
| | X. $5x$ |

**Riddle:** What can be a word, a number, a period of time, or a variable?

A _____ _____ . _____ _____

Holt Middle School Math   Course 2

Name _____ Date _____ Class _____

# Problem Solving
## *Combining Like Terms*

**Write the correct answer. Use the figures for Problems 1–3.**

1. Figure 1 shows the length of each side of a garden. Write an expression for the perimeter of the garden.

_____

2. Figure 2 is a square swimming pool. Write an expression to show the perimeter of the pool.

_____

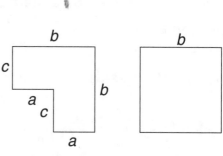

**Figure 1**          **Figure 2**

3. Write an expression for the combined perimeter of the garden and the pool.

_____

_____

4. The Pantheon in Rome has $n$ granite columns in each of 3 rows. Write an addition expression to show the number of columns, then combine like terms and evaluate the expression for $n = 8$.

_____

_____

**Choose the letter for the best answer.**

5. Which is an expression that shows the earnings of a telemarketer who worked for 23 hours at a salary of $d$ dollars per hour?

   **A** $d + 23$          **C** $d \div 23$

   **B** $23d$          **D** $23 \div d$

6. The minimum wage in 1997 was $5.15 per hour. Evaluate the expression $40h$ where $h = \$5.15$ to find a worker's weekly salary.

   **F** $20.60          **H** $515.00

   **G** $200          **J** $206.00

7. What is the perimeter of a triangle with sides the following lengths: $2a + 4c$, $3c + 7$, and $6a - 4$. Combine like terms in the expression.

   **A** $8a + 11c$

   **B** $6a + 7c + 3$

   **C** $8a + 7c + 3$

   **D** $8a + 7c + 11$

8. A hexagon is a 6-sided figure. Find the perimeter of a hexagon where all of the sides are the same length. The expression $x + y$ represents the length of a side. Combine like terms in the expression.

   **F** $6x + 6y$

   **G** $6 + x + y$

   **H** $6x + y$

   **J** $6xy$

Holt Middle School Math   Course 2

Name _____ Date _____ Class _____

**Write each verbal expression as an algebraic expression. Then
use the answer key to solve the riddle.**

**1.** the product of 20 and *t* _____

**2.** the sum of 4 times a number and 2 _____

**3.** the product of 7 and *p* _____

**4.** the sum of six times a number and 1 _____

**5.** the sum of 5 and a number _____

**6.** the quotient of a number and 8 _____

**7.** *m* plus 6 _____

**8.** *t* less than 23 _____

**9.** the quotient of 100 and the amount 6 plus *w* _____

**Answer Key**

| + | − | × | ÷ |
|---|---|---|---|
| S H<br>L B | N | G A | C I |

What's worse than raining cats and dogs?

___  ___  ___  ___  ___  ___  ___
 +    ×    ÷    +    ÷    −    ×

___  ___  ___  ___
 ÷    ×    +    +

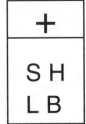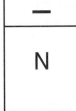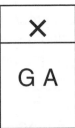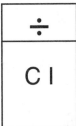

**Holt Middle School Math   Course 2**

# 2-10 Equations and Their Solutions

Marie spent $2. She has $5 left. How much did she have before she spent the $2?

The equation $x - 2 = 5$ represents the problem.

Because $7 - 2 = 5$ is a true statement, $x = 7$.

The solution to the equation $x - 2 = 5$ is 7, and the answer to the question is $7.

1. Make up three real-world problems that have 7 for an answer.

2. Write three equations that represent your problems in number 1.

## Think and Discuss _____

3. **Explain** what a solution to an equation is.
4. **Describe** how to determine whether 75 is a solution to the equation $25 = 100 - x$.

**This page is available as a transparency.**

Holt Middle School Math    Course 2

## Exploration Recording Sheet
**LESSON 2-10** *Equations and Their Solutions*

Marie spent $2. She has $5 left. How much did she have before she spent the $2?

The equation $x - 2 = 5$ represents the problem.

Because $7 - 2 = 5$ is a true statement, $x = 7$.

The solution to the equation $x - 2 = 5$ is 7, and the answer to the question is $7.

1. Make up three real-world problems that have 7 for an answer.

_____

_____

_____

_____

_____

2. Write three equations that represent your problems in number 1.


### Think and Discuss

3. **Explain** what a solution to an equation is.

_____

_____

4. **Describe** how to determine whether 75 is a solution to the equation $25 = 100 - x$.

_____

_____

_____

Holt Middle School Math   Course 2

Name _____ Date _____ Class _____

**Tell if each number is a solution of $n + 5 = 27$.**

**1.** 32                **2.** 22                **3.** 21                **4.** 34

_____      _____      _____      _____

**Tell if each number is a solution of $19 + a = 40$.**

**5.** 49                **6.** 31                **7.** 21                **8.** 39

_____      _____      _____      _____

**Tell if each number is a solution of $72 - x = 50$.**

**9.** 22                **10.** 122              **11.** 28               **12.** 18

_____      _____      _____      _____

**Tell if each number is a solution of $5 = 23 - w$.**

**13.** 28               **14.** 17               **15.** 13               **16.** 18

_____      _____      _____      _____

**17.** As of the 2000–2001 NBA season, Coach Phil Jackson had lost 234 games. This number is 434 fewer games than he won. The equation $234 = g - 434$ can be used to show the number of games Coach Jackson has won. Did he win 200, 464, or 668 games?

_____

**18.** Austin paid $350 for a new video game console. This is $125 more than a used console costs. The equation $350 = c + 125$ can be used to show the cost of a used video game console. Does a used console cost $225, $275, or $475?

_____

**19.** In the United States, there are 63 endangered species that are mammals. There are 15 more endangered species that are birds. Are there 78 or 48 endangered species of birds in the United States?

_____

**20.** At The Bike and Blade Shop, mountain bikes are on sale for $349. This is $30 more than a racing bike costs. Does the racing bike cost $319 or $379?

_____

Holt Middle School Math    Course 2

Name _____ Date _____ Class _____

**Determine if each number is a solution of $21 = x - 3$.**

**1.** 18          **2.** 26          **3.** 17          **4.** 24

_____   _____   _____   _____

**Determine if each number is a solution of $b + 19 = 52$.**

**5.** 71          **6.** 3          **7.** 33          **8.** 13

_____   _____   _____   _____

**Determine if the given numbers are solutions of the given equations.**

**9.** $k = 24$ for $3k = 6$          **10.** $m = 3$ for $42 = m + 39$   **11.** $y = 8$ for $8y + 6 = 70$

_____                    _____                    _____

**12.** $s = 5$ for $18 = 3s - 3$   **13.** $x = 7$ for $23 - k = 30$   **14.** $v = 12$ for $84 = 7v$

_____                    _____                    _____

**15.** $c = 15$ for $45 - 2c = 15$          **16.** $x = 10$ for $x + 25 - 2x + 4 = 19$

_____                              _____

**17.** $e = 6$ for $42 = 51 - e$          **18.** $p = 15$ for $19 = p - 4$

_____                              _____

**19.** $h = 9$ for $120 - 3h = 97$          **20.** $a = 25$ for $300 = 500 - 8a$

_____                              _____

**21.** Earth's diameter is about 7,926 miles. This is about 407 miles greater than the diameter of Venus. The equation $7,926 = v + 407$ can be used to represent the length of Venus' diameter. Is the diameter of Venus 8,333 miles or 7,519 miles?

**22.** Jason and Maya have their own Web sites on the Internet. As of last week, Jason's Web site had 2,426 visitors. This is twice as many visitors as Maya had. Did Maya have 1,213 visitors or 4,852 visitors to her Web site?

_____                    _____

**94**

Name _____ Date _____ Class _____

**Determine if the given numbers are solutions of the given equations.**

1. $a = 15$ for $75 \div a = 5$

_____

2. $x = 90$ for $x \div 9 = 100 - x$

_____

3. $d = 8$ for $875 = 909 - 4d$

_____

4. $x = 32$ for $2x - 25 + x - 70 = 1$

_____

5. $e = 2$ for $e^3 - e^2 = 6e - 8$

_____

6. $b = 4$ for $b^2 + 2b - 3 = 27$

_____

7. $d = 12$ for $4d - 24 - 12 = 0$

_____

8. $r = 9$ for $4r^2 - 19 - 5r = 340$

_____

9. $p = 25$ for $\frac{4p}{5} + 2p + 10 = 80$

_____

10. $t = 18$ for $\frac{t}{6} + \frac{54}{t} = 3$

_____

11. In 1991, there were about 7,200,000 cell phone subscribers in the United States. This is about 120,300,000 fewer subscribers than there were by the year 2001. The equation $7{,}200{,}000 = s - 120{,}300{,}000$ can be used to represent the number of cell phone subscribers in 2001. Were there 113,100,000 or 127,500,000 cell phone subscribers in the United States in 2001?

_____

12. Hector bought 50 shares of an Internet stock. He paid a commission of \$15. The total cost of the transaction was \$150. The equation $\$150 = 50n + 15$ can be used to represent the price Hector paid for each share of stock. Did he pay \$5.70, \$3.00, or \$2.70 per share of stock?

_____

13. The Super State Car Dealership has 120 mid-sized cars on the lot. There are half as many luxury cars as compact cars. There are 10 more pick-up trucks than luxury cars and half as many compact cars as mid-sized cars. Are there 40, 50, or 60 pick-up trucks on the lot of this car dealership?

_____

Holt Middle School Math   Course 2

Name _____ Date _____ Class _____

# Reteach
## *Equations and Their Solutions*

Number sentences that contain an equal sign (=) are called **equations**.

Equations may be true, or they may be false.

| True | False |
|---|---|
| 3 + 4 = 7 | 3 + 1 = 7 |
| 8 − 6 = 2 | 8 − 2 = 5 |

An equation may contain a variable.

**variable** → $x + 4 = 6$

Whether this equation is true or false depends on the value of *x*.

You can decide if a number is a *solution* of an equation. Substitute the number for the variable in the equation. If the equation is a true equation, then the number is the **solution.**

Equation: $x + 4 = 6$

Is 2 a solution?

$$x + 4 = 6$$

Substitute 2 for *x*

$$2 + 4 \overset{?}{=} 6$$

$$6 \overset{?}{=} 6 \qquad \text{True}$$

2 is a solution of $x + 4 = 6$.

Is 3 a solution?

$$x + 4 = 6$$

Substitute 3 for *x*

$$3 + 4 \overset{?}{=} 6$$

$$7 \overset{?}{=} 6 \qquad \text{False}$$

3 is not a solution of $x + 4 = 6$.

---

**Determine if the number is a solution of the equation.**

**1.** Is 3 a solution of $y + 3 = 9$?

_____

**2.** Is 4 a solution of $n + 6 = 10$?

_____

**3.** Is 2 a solution of $w − 1 = 1$?

_____

**4.** Is 1 a solution of $x + 50 = 49$?

_____

**5.** Is 6 a solution of $c + 23 = 30$?

_____

**6.** Is 9 a solution of $v − 9 = 0$?

_____

**7.** Is 20 a solution of $t − 17 = 3$?

_____

**8.** Is 16 a solution of $12 + a = 24$?

_____

**9.** Is 25 a solution of $38 − m = 13$?

_____

**10.** Is 8 a solution of $15 = e + 5$?

_____

Holt Middle School Math   Course 2

Name _____ Date _____ Class _____

# Challenge
## *The Solution Is BINGO!*

**Find the solution to each problem or equation. Cross it out on the board below to get BINGO!**

**1.** Is 37, 47, or 67 a solution for
$52 = n + 15$?

_____

**2.** Is 14, 17, or 21 a solution for
$8y - 7 = 129$?

_____

**3.** Is 14, 22, or 24 a solution for
$132 - (4x - 5) = 81$?

_____

**4.** Is 12, 15, or 18 a solution for
$3(60 - s) - 2s = 105$?

_____

**5.** Garret scored 18 points in his last basketball game, which is 6 fewer points than Vince scored. The equation $18 = p - 6$ can be used to represent Vince's points. Did Vince score 12, 24, or 28 points?

_____

**6.** In 3 years, Sarah's sister will be twice as old as Sarah. If Sarah is now 3 years old, will her sister be 6, 9, or 12 years old in 3 years?

_____

**7.** The highest recorded temperature in Alaska was 100°F in 1915. This was 56 years before the lowest recorded temperature of −80°F. Was the lowest recorded temperature in 1856, 1956, or 1971?

_____

**8.** In 1999, Florida had 2,145 elementary schools. This was 288 fewer elementary schools than 3 times the number of elementary schools in South Carolina during the same year. Did South Carolina have 427, 811, or 1,857 elementary schools in 1999?

_____

| B | I | N | G | O |
|---|---|---|---|---|
| 17 | 67 | 24 | 37 | 1971 |
| 6 | 24 | 47 | 1,857 | 22 |
| 427 | 1956 | FREE | 18 | 14 |
| 12 | 9 | 16 | 811 | 1856 |
| 28 | 23 | 21 | 19 | 15 |

Holt Middle School Math    Course 2

# Problem Solving

LESSON
**2-10** *Equations and Their Solutions*

**Write the correct answer.**

1. The jet airplane was invented in 1939. This is 12 years after the first television was invented. Was television invented in 1927 or 1951?

_____

2. There are three times as many students in the high school as in the junior high school, which has 330 students. Does the high school have 990 students or 110 students?

_____

3. The frigate bird has been recorded at speeds up to 95 mi/h. The only faster bird ever recorded was the spine-tailed swift at 11 mi/h faster. Was the speed of the spine-tailed swift 84 mi/h or 106 mi/h?

_____

4. As of February 2000, 14.6 million households in Canada were online. This is 10.1 million more households online than in Australia. Were 24.7 million or 4.5 million households online in Australia?

_____

**Choose the letter for the best answer.**

5. In the United States, the average school year is 180 days. This is 71 days less than the average school year in China. What is the average school year in China?

A 251 days

B 109 days

C 151 days

D 271 days

6. The longest bridge in the world is the Akashi Kaikyo Bridge in Japan. Its main span is 1,290 feet longer than a mile. A mile is 5,280 feet. How long is the Akashi Kaikyo bridge?

F 3,990 feet

G 6,400 feet

H 4,049 feet

J 6,570 feet

7. *Ornithomimus* stood about 6 feet tall and was the fastest dinosaur at a speed of about 50 mi/h. The largest dinosaur, *Seismosaurus,* was 20 times as tall. How tall was *Seismosaurus?*

A 12 feet

B 70 feet

C 120 feet

D 26 feet

8. Milton collects sports trading cards. He has 80 baseball cards. He has half as many basketball cards as football cards. He has 20 more hockey cards than basketball cards and half as many football cards as baseball cards. How many hockey cards does he have?

F 20 hockey cards

G 40 hockey cards

H 60 hockey cards

J 80 hockey cards

Holt Middle School Math   Course 2

Name _____ Date _____ Class _____

## Puzzles, Twisters & Teasers
*The Answer Popped Right into My Head!*

Find the solution for each equation below. Write the letter on the line above the correct answer at the bottom of the page to solve the riddle.

P   $18 = s - 7$   _____

M   $x + 3 = 10$   _____

O   $12 = t + 9$   _____

Y   $s - 38 = 57$   _____

R   $16 - j = 12$   _____

I   $16 = 34 - m$   _____

U   $48 = x + 12$   _____

S   $17 + k = 40$   _____

N   $24 = 34 - n$   _____

B   $p + 18 = 29$   _____

A   $47 = v - 6$   _____

G   $94 = c + 6$   _____

H   $82 = j + 9$   _____

E   $a - 15 = 17$   _____

T   $15 = k - 9$   _____

What did one firecracker say to the other?

___  ___     ___  ___  ___     ___  ___
 7    95      25    3   25      18    23

___  ___  ___  ___  ___  ___     ___  ___  ___  ___
11   18   88   88   32    4      24   73   53   10

___  ___  ___  ___     ___  ___  ___.
95    3   36    4      25    3   25

**Holt Middle School Math   Course 2**

## 2-11 Solving Equations by Adding or Subtracting

Find a solution to each equation.

| Equations with Addition | Equations with Subtraction |
|---|---|
| **1.** $n + 100 = 135$ | **5.** $91 - n = 10$ |
| $n =$ _____ | $n =$ _____ |
| **2.** $10 + n = 91$ | **6.** $n - 10 = 43$ |
| $n =$ _____ | $n =$ _____ |
| **3.** $n + 25 = 75$ | **7.** $75 - n = 25$ |
| $n =$ _____ | $n =$ _____ |
| **4.** $13 + n = 23$ | **8.** $n - 15 = 23$ |
| $n =$ _____ | $n =$ _____ |

## Think and Discuss

9. **Discuss** your strategies for solving the equations.
10. **Describe** how the operations of addition and subtraction "undo" each other.

**This page is available as a transparency.**

Holt Middle School Math   Course 2

Name _____ Date _____ Class _____

# Exploration Recording Sheet
## Solving Equations by Adding or Subtracting

**Find a solution to each equation.**

| Equations with Addition | Equations with Subtraction |
|---|---|
| **1.** $n + 100 = 135$ | **5.** $91 - n = 10$ |
| $n =$ _____ | $n =$ _____ |
| **2.** $10 + n = 91$ | **6.** $n - 10 = 43$ |
| $n =$ _____ | $n =$ _____ |
| **3.** $n + 25 = 75$ | **7.** $75 - n = 25$ |
| $n =$ _____ | $n =$ _____ |
| **4.** $13 + n = 23$ | **8.** $n - 15 = 23$ |
| $n =$ _____ | $n =$ _____ |

## Think and Discuss

**9. Discuss** your strategies for solving the equations.

_____

_____

**10. Describe** how the operations of addition and subtraction "undo" each other.

_____

_____

Holt Middle School Math   **Course 2**

**Match each equation in Column A with its correct solution in Column B.**

| Column A | Column B | Column A | Column B |
|---|---|---|---|
| **1.** $n - 16 = 8$ | **A.** $n = 12$ | **10.** $x - 12 = 13$ | **L.** $x = 14$ |
| **2.** $5 = n - 7$ | **B.** $n = 13$ | **11.** $x + 8 = 40$ | **M.** $x = 17$ |
| **3.** $12 + n = 25$ | **C.** $n = 17$ | **12.** $34 = 16 + x$ | **N.** $x = 18$ |
| **4.** $n - 17 = 11$ | **D.** $n = 24$ | **13.** $x + 5 = 19$ | **P.** $x = 25$ |
| **5.** $n + 18 = 35$ | **E.** $n = 27$ | **14.** $4 + x = 52$ | **Q.** $x = 32$ |
| **6.** $7 = n - 28$ | **F.** $n = 28$ | **15.** $12 + x = 50$ | **R.** $x = 33$ |
| **7.** $n - 12 = 40$ | **G.** $n = 35$ | **16.** $15 = x - 2$ | **S.** $x = 38$ |
| **8.** $24 = n - 25$ | **H.** $n = 49$ | **17.** $52 = x + 9$ | **T.** $x = 43$ |
| **9.** $46 = n + 19$ | **J.** $n = 52$ | **18.** $x - 11 = 22$ | **U.** $x = 48$ |

**19.** Chris has 55 baseball trading cards. He has 17 more cards than his sister Sara has. Write and solve an equation to find how many trading cards Sara has.

_____

**20.** In 2000, Sammy Sosa hit 50 home runs. His home run total was 23 runs fewer than the number of home runs that Barry Bonds hit the next year. Write and solve an equation to find how many home runs Barry Bonds hit in 2001.

_____

Holt Middle School Math   Course 2

## LESSON Practice B
## 2-11 Solving Equations by Adding or Subtracting

**Solve the equation. Check your answer.**

**1.** $33 = y - 44$

**2.** $r - 32 = 77$

**3.** $125 = x - 29$

_____

_____

_____

**4.** $k + 18 = 25$

**5.** $589 + x = 700$

**6.** $96 = 56 + t$

_____

_____

_____

**7.** $a - 9 = 57$

**8.** $b - 49 = 254$

**9.** $987 = f - 11$

_____

_____

_____

**10.** $32 + d = 1,400$

**11.** $w - 24 = 90$

**12.** $95 = g - 340$

_____

_____

_____

**13.** $e - 35 = 59$

**14.** $84 = v + 30$

**15.** $h + 15 = 81$

_____

_____

_____

**16.** $110 = a + 25$

**17.** $45 + c = 91$

**18.** $p - 29 = 78$

_____

_____

_____

**19.** $56 - r = 8$

**20.** $39 = z + 8$

**21.** $93 + g = 117$

_____

_____

_____

**22.** The Morales family is driving from Philadelphia to Boston. So far, they have driven 167 miles. This is 129 miles less than the total distance they must travel. How many miles is Philadelphia from Boston?

_____

**23.** Ron has $1,230 in his savings account. This is $400 more than he needs to buy a new big screen TV. Write and solve an equation to find out how much the TV costs.

_____

Holt Middle School Math   Course 2

## Practice C

**LESSON 2-11** *Solving Equations by Adding or Subtracting*

**Solve the equation. Check your answer.**

**1.** $b - 32 = 15$

**2.** $e - 43 = 121$

**3.** $601 = x - 24$

_____

_____

_____

**4.** $m + 45 = 123$

**5.** $314 + z = 350$

**6.** $840 = 45 + f$

_____

_____

_____

**7.** $d - 67 = 23$

**8.** $w + 233 = 319$

**9.** $91 = x + 52$

_____

_____

_____

**10.** $150 + y = 879$

**11.** $k - 32 = 217$

**12.** $408 = s - 129$

_____

_____

_____

**13.** $108 = j - 24$

**14.** $1{,}204 = w + 389$

**15.** $p - 167 = 321$

_____

_____

_____

**16.** In 2000, the *Wall Street Journal* was the leading U.S. daily newspaper, with a circulation of 1,762,751. This was 70,085 more than the second leading daily newspaper, *USA Today*. Write and solve an equation to find the circulation of *USA Today* in 2000.

_____

**17.** Mrs. Baker's class has been raising money for a local charity. At the end of last week, they had collected $238. By the end of this week, they had a total of $419. Write and solve an equation to find the amount collected this week.

_____

**18.** Andy Green broke the sound barrier on land on October 15, 1997, in Black Rock Desert, Nevada. The speed of sound was recorded at about 751 mi/h. This was about 12 mi/h less than the land speed record that he set that day. Write and solve an equation to find Andy Green's land speed record.

_____

Holt Middle School Math   Course 2

Name _____ Date _____ Class _____

Solving an equation is like balancing a scale. If you add the same weight to both sides of a balanced scale, the scale will remain balanced. You can use this same idea to solve an equation.

Think of the equation $x - 7 = 12$ as a balanced scale. The equal sign keeps the balance.

$$x - 7 = 12$$

$\boxed{-7 + 7 = 0}$ $\quad x - 7 + 7 = 12 + 7$ $\quad$ Add 7 to both sides.
$$x + 0 = 19 \quad\quad \text{Combine like terms.}$$
$$x = 19$$

When you solve an equation, the idea is to get the variable by itself. What you do to one side of the equation, you must do to the other side.

• To solve a subtraction equation, use addition.

• To solve an addition equation, use subtraction.

Solve and check: $y + 8 = 14$.

$$y + 8 = 14$$

$\boxed{+8 - 8 = 0}$ $\quad y + 8 - 8 = 14 - 8$ $\quad$ Subtract 8 from both sides.
$$y + 0 = 6 \quad\quad \text{Combine like terms.}$$
$$y = 6$$

**Check:** $\quad y + 8 = 14 \quad\quad$ To check, substitute 6 for $y$.
$$6 + 8 \stackrel{?}{=} 14$$
$$14 \stackrel{?}{=} 14 \quad ✔$$

A true sentence, $14 = 14$, means the solution is correct.

---

**Solve and check.**

1. $\quad\quad x - 2 = 8$

$\quad x - 2 + \underline{\quad} = 8 + \underline{\quad}$

$\quad\quad x - 0 = \underline{\quad}$

2. $\quad\quad b + 5 = 11$

$\quad b + 5 - \underline{\quad} = 11 - \underline{\quad}$

$\quad\quad b + 0 = \underline{\quad}$

3. $n + 8 = 11$ $\quad\quad$ 4. $y - 6 = 2$ $\quad\quad$ 5. $a - 9 = 4$ $\quad\quad$ 6. $m + 2 = 18$

_____ $\quad$ _____ $\quad$ _____ $\quad$ _____

Holt Middle School Math **Course 2**

## LESSON 2-11 **Challenge**
*Equation Maker*

**Use each term once to make up one addition and one subtraction equation, then solve the equations.**

**1.** *m, n*, 12, 6, 54, 9

_____

_____

**2.** *x, y*, 7, 15, 32, 45

_____

_____

**3.** *p, q*, 19, 44, 72, 8

_____

_____

**4.** *a, b*, 67, 102, 6, 8

_____

_____

**5.** *c, d*, 11, 12, 18, 35

_____

_____

**6.** *s, t*, 115, 123, 32, 0

_____

_____

**7.** *w, y*, 1, 2, 3, 4

_____

_____

**8.** *n, p*, 6, 22, 99, 400

_____

_____

**9.** *e, f*, 52, 4, 75, 18

_____

_____

**10.** *g, h*, 61, 88, 94, 117

_____

_____

**11.** *k, l*, 302, 54, 115, 79

_____

_____

**12.** *r, s*, 90, 14, 71, 15

_____

_____

**13.** *u, v*, 8, 12, 37, 44

_____

_____

**14.** *x, y*, 198, 0, 231, 4

_____

_____

Holt Middle School Math   Course 2

Name _____ Date _____ Class _____

LESSON **Problem Solving**
**2-11** *Solving Equations by Adding or Subtracting*

**Write the correct answer.**

1. In an online poll, 1,927 people voted for Coach as the best job at the Super Bowl. The job of Announcer received 8,055 more votes. Write and solve an equation to find how many votes the job of Announcer received.

2. In 2001, the largest bank in the world was Mizuho Holdings, Japan, with $1,295 billion in assets. This was $351 billion more than the largest bank in the United States, Citigroup. Write and solve an equation to find Citigroup's assets.

_____

_____

3. The two smallest countries in the world are Vatican City and Monaco. Vatican City is 1.37 square kilometers smaller than Monaco, which is 1.81 square kilometers in area. What is the area of Vatican City?

4. The Library of Congress is the largest library in the world. It has 24 million books, which is 8 million more than the National Library of Canada has. How many books does the National Library of Canada have?

_____

_____

**Choose the letter for the best answer.**

5. The first track on Sean's new CD has been playing for 55 seconds. This is 42 seconds less than the time of the entire first track. How long is the first track on this CD?

   **A** 37 seconds       **C** 97 seconds

   **B** 63 seconds       **D** 93 seconds

6. There are 45 students on the school football team. This is 13 more than the number of students on the basketball team. How many students are on the basketball team?

   **F** 58 students       **H** 32 students

   **G** 48 students       **J** 42 students

7. A used mountain bike costs $79.95. This is $120 less than the cost of a new one. If $c$ is the cost of the new bike, which equation can you use to find the cost of a new bike?

   **A** $79.95 = c + 120$

   **B** $120 = 79.95 - c$

   **C** $79.95 = c - 120$

   **D** $120 = 79.95 + c$

8. The goal of the School Bake Sale is to raise $125 more than last year's sale. Last year the Bake Sale raised $320. If it reaches its goal, how much will the Bake Sale raise this year?

   **F** $445

   **G** $195

   **H** $525

   **J** $425

Holt Middle School Math   Course 2

Name _____ Date _____ Class _____

# Puzzles, Twisters & Teasers

## *Clean Solutions!*

Find the solution for each equation below. Write the letter of
each variable on the line above the correct answer at the
bottom of the page to solve the riddle.

**1.** $y - 35 = 17$ _____

**2.** $h - 40 = 26$ _____

**3.** $a + 16 = 43$ _____

**4.** $110 = e + 66$ _____

**5.** $97 = w - 44$ _____

**6.** $n - 8 = 3$ _____

**7.** $356 = g - 218$ _____

**8.** $652 + t = 800$ _____

**9.** $16 = a - 124$ _____

**10.** $63 + m = 903$ _____

**11.** $k + 18 = 98$ _____

**12.** $d - 27 = 54$ _____

**13.** $c - 50 = 23$ _____

**14.** $l - 62 = 937$ _____

Why did the robber take a shower?

___ ___   ___ ___ ___ ___ ___ ___   ___ ___
66  44    141 27  11  148 44  81    148 140

___ ___ ___ ___   ___   ___ ___ ___ ___ ___
840 27  80  44    27    73  999 44  27  11

___ ___ ___   ___ ___ ___ ___ .
574 44  148   27  141 27  52

Holt Middle School Math   Course 2

# 2-12 Solving Equations by Multiplying or Dividing

Find a solution to each equation.

**Equations with Multiplication** | **Equations with Division**

**1.** $n \cdot 4 = 56$

$n =$ _____

**2.** $13 \cdot n = 65$

$n =$ _____

**3.** $n \cdot 15 = 75$

$n =$ _____

**4.** $25 \cdot n = 525$

$n =$ _____

**5.** $n \div 5 = 100$

$n =$ _____

**6.** $75 \div n = 15$

$n =$ _____

**7.** $n \div 2 = 75$

$n =$ _____

**8.** $125 \div n = 25$

$n =$ _____

## Think and Discuss

**9. Discuss** your strategies for solving the equations.

**10. Describe** how the operations of multiplication and division "undo" each other.

This page is available as a transparency.

Name _____ Date _____ Class _____

# Exploration Recording Sheet
## *Solving Equations by Multiplying or Dividing*

**Find a solution to each equation.**

Equations with Multiplication | Equations with Division

**1.** $n \cdot 4 = 56$

$n =$ _____

**2.** $13 \cdot n = 65$

$n =$ _____

**3.** $n \cdot 15 = 75$

$n =$ _____

**4.** $25 \cdot n = 525$

$n =$ _____

**5.** $n \div 5 = 100$

$n =$ _____

**6.** $75 \div n = 15$

$n =$ _____

**7.** $n \div 2 = 75$

$n =$ _____

**8.** $125 \div n = 25$

$n =$ _____

## Think and Discuss

**9. Discuss** your strategies for solving the equations.

_____

_____

**10. Describe** how the operations of multiplication and division "undo" each other.

_____

_____

Holt Middle School Math   Course 2

**Practice A**

*Solving Equations by Multiplying or Dividing*

**Solve.**

**1.** $16 = n \div 2$

**2.** $\frac{e}{10} = 8$

**3.** $25 = \frac{x}{6}$

_____    _____    _____

**4.** $18 = \frac{d}{3}$

**5.** $a \div 12 = 7$

**6.** $30 = b \div 4$

_____    _____    _____

**Solve and check.**

**7.** $7w = 49$

**8.** $75 = 3x$

**9.** $60 = 12p$

_____    _____    _____

**10.** $77 = 11m$

**11.** $4h = 48$

**12.** $9y = 54$

_____    _____    _____

**13.** $2x = 30$

**14.** $45 = 5s$

**15.** $6z = 42$

_____    _____    _____

**16.** The Fruit Stand charges $0.50 each for navel oranges. Kareem paid $4.00 for a large bag of navel oranges. How many did he buy?

_____

**17.** Jenny can type at a speed of 80 words per minute. It took her 20 minutes to type a report. How many words was the report?

_____

**18.** At the local gas station, regular unleaded gasoline is priced at $1.10 per gallon. If it cost $16.50 to fill a car's gas tank, how many gallons of gasoline did the tank hold?

_____

Holt Middle School Math    Course 2

**LESSON** **Practice B**
**2-12** *Solving Equations by Multiplying or Dividing*

**Solve the equation.**

**1.** $68 = \dfrac{r}{4}$

**2.** $k \div 24 = 85$

**3.** $255 = \dfrac{x}{4}$

_____

_____

_____

**4.** $42 = w \div 18$

**5.** $\dfrac{a}{15} = 22$

**6.** $82 = b \div 5$

_____

_____

_____

**7.** $\dfrac{c}{7} = 9$

**8.** $28 = z \div 3$

**9.** $\dfrac{y}{12} = 10$

_____

_____

_____

**Solve the equation. Check the answer.**

**10.** $52w = 364$

**11.** $41x = 492$

**12.** $410 = 82p$

_____

_____

_____

**13.** $35d = 735$

**14.** $195 = 65h$

**15.** $4k = 140$

_____

_____

_____

**16.** $110 = 5e$

**17.** $27a = 216$

**18.** $96 = 12n$

_____

_____

_____

**19.** Ashley earns $5.50 per hour babysitting. She wants to buy a CD player that costs $71.50, including tax. How many hours will she need to work to earn the money for the CD player?

_____

**20.** A cat can jump the height of up to 5 times the length of its tail. Write and solve an equation to show the height a cat can jump if its tail is 13 inches long.

_____

_____

Holt Middle School Math   **Course 2**

Name _____ Date _____ Class _____

**Solve the equation. Check the answer.**

**1.** $765 = \frac{n}{12}$          **2.** $\frac{m}{9} = 26$          **3.** $\frac{a}{12} = 14$

_____          _____          _____

**4.** $3g = 165$          **5.** $308 = 44b$          **6.** $27e = 405$

_____          _____          _____

**Translate the sentence into an equation. Then solve the equation.**

**7.** The product of a number $w$ and 145 is 725.  _____

**8.** The quotient of a number $f$ and 21 is 14.  _____

**9.** A number $b$ times 23 equals 253.  _____

**10.** A number $k$ divided by 15 equals 47.  _____

**11.** A number $n$ multiplied by 12 is 84.  _____

**12.** Ten divided into a number $m$ equals 54.  _____

**13.** About three tons of ore must be mined and processed to produce a single ounce of gold. How many tons of ore are required to produce a pound of gold?

_____

**14.** It costs about $2,931 per hour to operate a Boeing 757 airplane. Find the cost to operate a Boeing 757 during a 5-hour flight.

_____

**15.** Each person in the United States eats an average of 23 quarts of ice cream per year. At this rate, Ms. Diamond's seventh-grade class will eat about 1,794 quarts of ice cream this year. How many students are in Ms. Diamond's seventh-grade class?

_____

**16.** Jumbo shrimp sell for $14.99 per pound in a local supermarket. One customer spent $74.95 on shrimp for a dinner party. How much shrimp did this customer purchase for the party?

_____

                   **Holt Middle School Math   Course 2**

Name _____ Date _____ Class _____

## Reteach
### *Solving Equations by Multiplying or Dividing*

When you solve an equation, you must get the variable by itself. Remember, what you do to one side of an equation, you must do to the other side.

- To solve a division equation, multiply both sides of the equation by the same number.

Solve and check: $\frac{a}{3} = 4$.

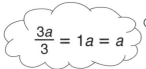

$$\frac{a}{3} = 4$$

$$(3)\frac{a}{3} = 4(3)$$

$$a = 12$$

Multiply to solve a division equation.

**Check:**  $\frac{a}{3} = 4$

$$\frac{12}{3} \stackrel{?}{=} 4$$

$$4 \stackrel{?}{=} 4 \quad ✔$$

Replace the variable with the solution.

A true sentence means the solution is correct.

**Solve and check.**

**1.** $\frac{x}{6} = 3$  **2.** $\frac{s}{8} = 8$  **3.** $\frac{c}{10} = 7$  **4.** $\frac{n}{3} = 12$

_____ _____ _____ _____

- To solve a multiplication equation, divide both sides of the equation by the same number.

Solve and check: $5k = 30$.

$$\frac{5k}{5} = 1k = k$$

$$5k = 30$$

$$\frac{5k}{5} = \frac{30}{5}$$

$$k = 6$$

Divide to solve a multiplication equation.

**Check:** $5k = 30$

$$5(6) \stackrel{?}{=} 30$$

$$30 \stackrel{?}{=} 30 \quad ✔$$

True

Replace the variable with the solution.

**Solve and check.**

**5.** $2w = 16$  **6.** $4b = 24$  **7.** $9z = 45$  **8.** $10m = 40$

_____ _____ _____ _____

**Holt Middle School Math   Course 2**

Name _____ Date _____ Class _____

# Challenge
## *Shape Up*

**Find the value of each shape in Exercises 1–8. Then use the values to answer the questions below.**

**1.**

2 🦋 = 32

4 🐝 = 🦋

🦋 = __ ; 🐝 = __

**2.**

3 🥁 = 18

2 🪘 = 🥁

🥁 = __ ; 🪘 = __

**3.**

4 ✳ = 8

2 🪁 = ✳

✳ = __ ; 🪁 = __

**4.**

12 ☆ = 108

3 ☾ = ☆

☆ = __ ; ☾ = __

**5.**

24 🐚 = 192

32 🐚 = 0

🐚 = __ ; 🐚 = __

**6.**

39 🌺 = 117

3 🍃 = 🌺

🌺 = __ ; 🍃 = __

**7.**

4 🍎 = 🍌 + 🍐

🍌 = 🍐 + 🍎

2 🍌 = 30

🍌 = __ ; 🍎 = __ ; 🍐 = __

**8.**

2 ⬭ = △

5 ⬡ = ⬭ + △

3 ⬭ = 15

⬭ = __ ; △ = __ ; ⬡ = __

**9.** What was the population of the United States in 1610?

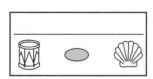

**10.** What was the population of the United States in 2000?

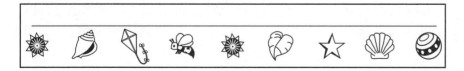

Name _____ Date _____ Class _____

# Problem Solving
## Solving Equations by Multiplying or Dividing

**Write the correct answer.**

1. The Panama Canal cost $387,000,000 to build. Each ship pays $34,000 to pass through the canal. How many ships had to pass through the canal to pay for the cost to build it?

_____

_____

2. The rate of exchange for currency changes daily. One day you could get $25 for 3,302.75 Japanese yen. Write and solve a multiplication equation to find the number of yen per dollar on that day.

_____

_____

3. Franklin D. Roosevelt was in office as president for 12 years. This is three times as long as Jimmy Carter was president. Write and solve an equation to show how long Jimmy Carter was president.

_____

4. The mileage from Dallas to Miami is 1,332 miles. To the nearest hour, how many hours would it take to drive from Dallas to Miami at an average speed of 55 mi/h?

_____

**Choose the letter for the best answer.**

5. The total bill for a bike rental for 8 hours was $38. How much per hour was the rental cost?

   A  $8 per hour

   B  $4.75 per hour

   C  $30 per hour

   D  $5.25 per hour

6. If a salesclerk earns $5.75 per hour, how many hours per week does she work to earn her weekly salary of $207?

   F  30 hours

   G  32 hours

   H  36 hours

   J  4 hours

7. At a cost of $0.07 per minute, which equation could you use to find out how many minutes you can talk for $3.15?

   A  $0.07 \div m = $3.15$

   B  $3.15 \cdot m = $0.07$

   C  $0.07m = $3.15$

   D  $0.07 \div $3.15 = m$

8. Which equation shows how to find a runner's distance if he ran a total of $m$ miles in 36 minutes at an average of a mile every 7.2 minutes?

   F  $36 \div m = 7.2$

   G  $7.2 \div m = 36$

   H  $36m = 7.2$

   J  $7.2 \div 36 = m$

Holt Middle School Math   Course 2

## LESSON 2-12 Puzzles, Twisters & Teasers
### Doctor! Doctor!

Find the solution for each equation below. Write the letter of each variable on the line above the correct answer at the bottom of the page to solve the riddle.

**1.** $a \div 25 = 4$ _____

**2.** $w \times 18 = 18$ _____

**3.** $r \div 8 = 5$ _____

**4.** $3h = 96$ _____

**5.** $72 = 8d$ _____

**6.** $12 = y \div 4$ _____

**7.** $17 = n \div 8$ _____

**8.** $85 = 17o$ _____

**9.** $3e = 63$ _____

**10.** $9 = u \div 3$ _____

**11.** $6b = 222$ _____

**12.** $7m = 84$ _____

**13.** $150 = 3t$ _____

**14.** $9s = 99$ _____

Patient: Doctor! Doctor! I feel like an umbrella!

Doctor: ___ ___ ___ ,    ___ ___ ___
     1   32  48      48   5   27

   ___ ___ ___ ___    ___ ___
   12  27  11  50    37  21

   ___ ___ ___ ___ ___    ___ ___ ___
   27  136  9  21  40    50  32  21

   ___ ___ ___ ___ ___ ___ ___ .
   1  21  100  50  32  21  40

Holt Middle School Math   Course 2

Name _____ Date _____ Class _____

### 2-1 Exponents (pp. 60–63)
Find each value.

**1.** $7^3$ _____  **2.** $4^5$ _____  **3.** $6^4$ _____

Write each number using an exponent and the given base.

**4.** 64, base 8 _____  **5.** 125, base 5 _____  **6.** 900, base 30 _____

### 2-2 Powers of Ten and Scientific Notation (pp. 64–67)
Find each product.

**7.** $42 \times 10^3$ _____  **8.** $17 \times 10^1$ _____  **9.** $26.7 \times 10^4$ _____

Write each number in scientific notation.

**10.** 42,600,000 _____  **11.** 43,000 _____

### 2-3 Order of Operations (pp. 70–74)
Evaluate.

**12.** $42 - 5 \times 4 + 3$  **13.** $5 \times 7 - 18 \div 3$  **14.** $5 + (28 \div 7)^2 \div 2$

_____   _____   _____

**15.** To raise money for charity, Leslie got pledges from her family. For the first 10 miles that she bikes, she will receive $15, then 50 cents for every mile that she completes after that. If she bikes 32 miles, how much money should she collect?

**16.** Ben spent $6 per square foot for tile for a counter top and $32 for glue and grout. Evaluate the expression $6(24 \times 60) \div 12^2 + \$32$ to find out how much he spent to tile a 24 in. by 60 in. counter top for a kitchen.

_____   _____

### 2-4 Prime Factorization (pp. 78–81)
Use a factor tree to find the prime factorization.

**17.** 12 _____  **18.** 42 _____

Use a step diagram to prime factor.

**19.** 196  **20.** 320

_____   _____

Holt Middle School Math   Course 2

| CHAPTER | **Review** |
|---|---|
| **2** | *Number Theory and Algebraic Reasoning (continued)* |

## 2-5 **Greatest Common Factor** (pp. 82–85)
**Find the greatest common factor (GCF).**

**21.** 35, 135 _____   **22.** 12, 48 _____   **23.** 16, 24, 64 _____

**24.** A hospital auxiliary is making identical get-well vases of flowers for their patients. They have 128 carnations and 96 roses. What is the greatest number of vases they can fill using all of the flowers?

_____

## 2-6 **Least Common Multiple** (pp. 86–90)
**Find the least common multiple (LCM).**

**25.** 4, 18 _____   **26.** 8, 14 _____   **27.** 5, 13, 20, 26 _____

**28.** A band is practicing for a competition. In the song, a xylophone player plays every fifth beat, and the drummer strikes his drum every sixth beat. When will the xylophone and the drum play the same beat?

_____

## 2-7 **Variables and Algebraic Expressions** (pp. 92–95)
**Evaluate $n + 12$ for each value of $n$.**

**29.** $n = 4$ _____   **30.** $n = 12$ _____   **31.** $n = 6$ _____

**Evaluate each algebraic expression for the given variables.**

**32.** $6x^2 + 2x + 1$ for $x = 2$ _____   **33.** $3a + 8a - 9$ for $a = 4$ _____

## 2-8 **Translate Words Into Math** (pp. 96–99)
**Write as an algebraic expression.**

**34.** 3 less than the product of 9 and a number _____

**35.** the sum of 6 times a number and 3 _____

Holt Middle School Math   Course 2

| CHAPTER | Review |
|---|---|
| **2** | *Number Theory and Algebraic Reasoning (continued)* |

## 2-9 Combining Like Terms (pp. 100–103)
Combine the like terms.

**36.** $6a + 4b + 9a$

_____

**37.** $2a + 2b + 3a + 4b + 7$

_____

**38.** $11 + 9x^2 + x + 4$

_____

**39.** $4a + 6b - 3a + b + 1$

_____

## 2-10 Equations and Their Solutions (pp. 104–107)
Determine if each number is a solution of $n - 6 = 28$.

**40.** $n = 42$ _____

**41.** $n = 34$ _____

**42.** $n = 22$ _____

**43.** Jeremy has saved $234 to buy a DVD player, which is $29 less than he needs. Does the DVD player cost $263 or $205?

**44.** Brenda and Cindy are making necklaces. Brenda has 36 beads. This is 8 more than Cindy. The equation $36 = x + 8$ can be used to represent the total number of beads. Does Cindy have 44, 25, or 28 beads?

_____

_____

## 2-11 Solving Equations by Adding or Subtracting (pp. 110–113)
Solve each equation.

**45.** $109 = x + 27$

_____

**46.** $y - 38 = 87$

_____

**47.** $a + 17 = 50$

_____

**48.** Robin is reading a 310 page book. She has read 275 pages so far. How many pages does she have yet to read?

_____

## 2-12 Solving Equations by Multiplying or Dividing (pp. 114–117)
Solve each equation. Check your solution.

**49.** $\frac{n}{16} = 9$

_____

**50.** $23x = 115$

_____

**51.** $15 = y \div 3$

_____

**52.** Darren wants to buy a new lawn mower for his business. If the mower costs $350 and he can save $50 per week, how many weeks will it take Darren to save the money for the mower?

_____

Holt Middle School Math   Course 2

## Project Recording Sheet

**CHAPTER 2**  *Number Theory and Algebraic Reasoning*

**Space Spaces**

Use the table to construct a model that demonstrates the distances from the Sun to the planets, nearest star, and nearest galaxy.

Tip: One benefit of using exponents is that it makes it easier to compare numbers. For example:

Compare $1 \times 10^6$ and $1 \times 10^7$.
Convert $1 \times 10^7$ to $10 \times 10^6$.
$1 \times 10^7$ is ten times as large as $1 \times 10^6$.

**Complete the table to express all the distances using a common exponent.**

| Object | Average Distance from the Sun (km) | Average Distance from the Sun Expressed with a Common Exponent (km) |
|---|---|---|
| Mercury | $5.80 \times 10^7$ | |
| Venus | $1.082 \times 10^8$ | |
| Earth | $1.495 \times 10^8$ | |
| Mars | $2.279 \times 10^8$ | |
| Jupiter | $7.780 \times 10^8$ | |
| Saturn | $1.43 \times 10^9$ | |
| Uranus | $2.90 \times 10^9$ | |
| Neptune | $4.40 \times 10^9$ | |
| Pluto | $5.80 \times 10^9$ | |
| Nearest Star | $3.973 \times 10^{13}$ | |
| Nearest Galaxy | $1.514 \times 10^{18}$ | |

What problems did you have with your model or drawing? Was it possible to create a model with every space object? Why or why not?

_____

_____

**Extension:** Create a model or drawing showing the relative diameters of the planets.

_____

_____

## Teacher Support for Chapter Project

**CHAPTER 2**

*Number Theory and Algebraic Reasoning*

**Grade 7, Chapter 2:** Number Theory and Algebraic Reasoning

**Career:** Astronomer

### Background
Students will use exponents in order to solve problems.

### Lesson Connections
2-1, 2-2

### Answers to Research Questions

• Students will discover that the nearest star and galaxy will not fit into a scale that shows the relative distances between the Sun and the planets. Have them create a model for the planets and then estimate how far away the nearest star and galaxy would be at the scale used in the model.

• The diameters of the Sun and the planets are: Sun: 1,392,530 km; Mercury: 4,878 km; Venus: 12,104 km; Earth: 12,756 km; Mars: 6,794 km; Jupiter: 142,800 km; Saturn: 120,000 km; Uranus: 52,000 km; Neptune: 48,400 km.

• One light year is the distance that light travels through space in one year. At 300,000 ($3.0 \times 10^5$) km/s light travels $9.5 \times 10^{12}$ km in a year. (The Andromeda Galaxy is $2.3 \times 10^6$ l.y. from Earth.)

| Assessment Rubric | |
|---|---|
| 4 | Successfully created a model of the relative diameters of the planets. Explained the reasons for the difficulties of modeling all the space objects at one scale. |
| 3 | Successfully created an accurate model showing the relative distances between all the space objects. Partially explained the reasons for the difficulties of modeling all the space objects at one scale. |
| 2 | Successfully created an accurate model showing the relative distances between all the space objects. Did not explain the reasons for the difficulties of modeling all the space objects at one scale. |
| 1 | Created a model that was only partially accurate. |

Name _____ Date _____ Class _____

CHAPTER
2
# List of Teacher Tools
## *Number Theory and Algebraic Reasoning*

These are the Teacher Tools and manipulatives needed for the lessons in the student book, teacher book, and worksheets for this chapter.

| Lesson or Feature | | Teacher Tool in CRB | Found in Manipulative Kit |
|---|---|---|---|
| Lesson 1 Motivate (TE) | 10 x 10 grids [TR66] | X | |
| Lesson 1 Teaching Tip (TE) | Calculator | | |
| Lesson 2 Exploration | Calculator | | |
| Lesson 3 Exploration | Calculator | | |
| Lesson 3 Reaching All Learners (TE) | Recording sheet | X | |
| Lesson 4 Motivate (TE) | Grid paper [TR65] | X | |
| Lesson 5 Motivate (TE) | Two-color counters | | X |
| Lesson 6 Motivate | Calendar for September 2004 | X | |
| Lesson 7 Reaching All Learners (TE) | Recording sheet | X | |
| Lesson 9 Reaching All Learners (TE) | Algebra tiles [TR21] | X | X |

Holt Middle School Math   Cour'

Name _____ Date _____ Class _____

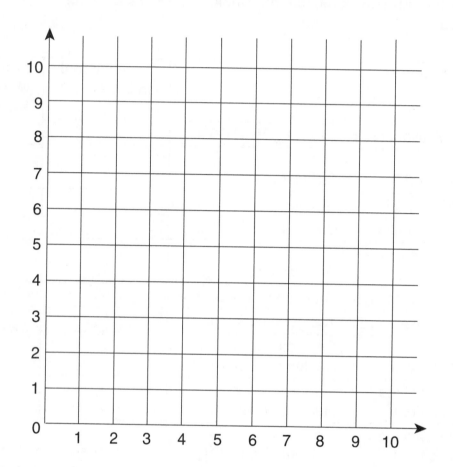

Name _____ Date _____ Class _____

**Decide which operation sign belongs in each box to make the number sentences true. You may need to use different operations more than once in each number sentence.**

1. Operation signs: +, −, •

   Number sentence:  12    4    6    3    7 = 37

   _____

2. Operation signs: ÷, +, −

   Number sentence:  18    2    24    12    4 = 22

   _____

Name _____ Date _____ Class _____

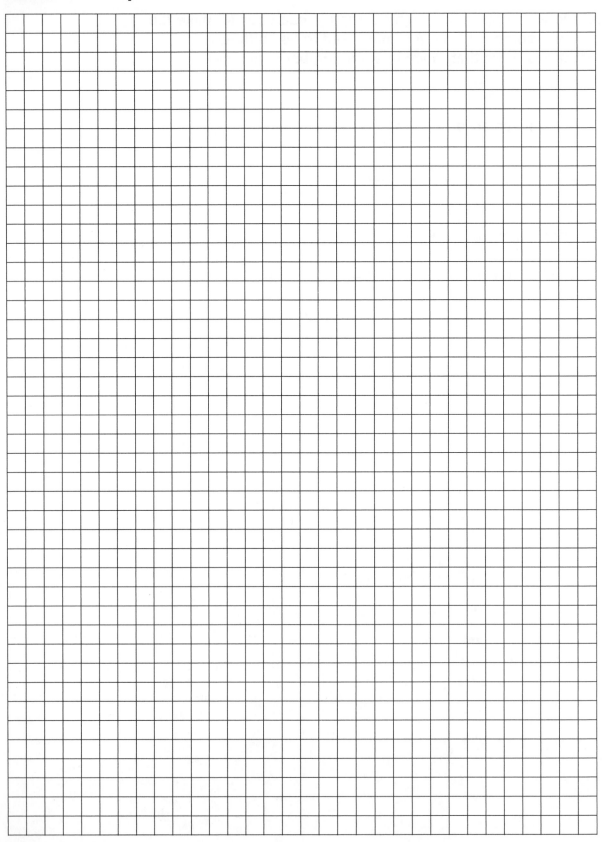

CHAPTER
2

**Teacher Tools**

*Grid Paper*

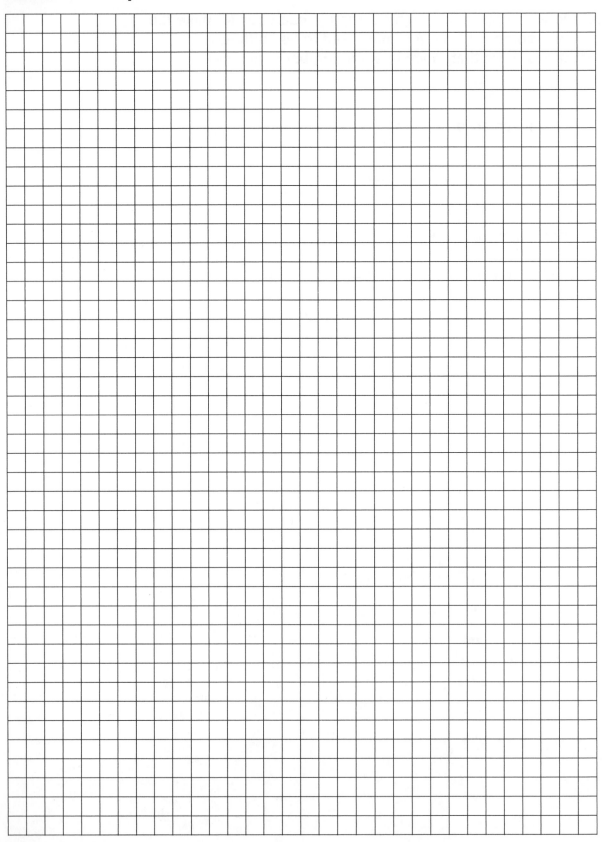

**Holt Middle School Math   Course 2**

Name _____ Date _____ Class _____

**Teacher Tools**
*Calendar*

| September 2004 | | | | | | |
|---|---|---|---|---|---|---|
| Sunday | Monday | Tuesday | Wednesday | Thursday | Friday | Saturday |
| | | | 1 | 2 | 3 | 4 |
| 5 | 6 | 7 | 8 | 9 | 10 | 11 |
| 12 | 13 | 14 | 15 | 16 | 17 | 18 |
| 19 | 20 | 21 | 22 | 23 | 24 | 25 |
| 26 | 27 | 28 | 29 | 30 | | |

Holt Middle School Math   Course 2

## LESSON 7 Recording Sheet for Reaching All Learners
### Variables and Algebraic Expressions

A magic square is an array of numbers in which each row, column, or diagonal has the same sum.

Decide if this is a magic square if $x = 4$, if $x = 6$, and if $x = 0$.

| | | |
|---|---|---|
| $x + 7$ | $x$ | $2x + 1$ |
| $x + 2$ | $0.5x + 6$ | $x + 6$ |
| $3x - 5$ | $3x$ | $x + 1$ |

Holt Middle School Math   Course 2

Name _____ Date _____ Class _____

# Teacher Tools
## *Algebra Tiles*

| 1 | 1 | 1 | 1 | 1 | 1 | 1 | 1 | 1 | 1 | 1 | 1 | 1 | 1 | 1 | 1 |
|---|---|---|---|---|---|---|---|---|---|---|---|---|---|---|---|
| 1 | 1 | 1 | 1 | 1 | 1 | 1 | 1 | 1 | 1 | 1 | 1 | 1 | 1 | 1 | 1 |
| 1 | 1 | 1 | 1 | 1 | 1 | 1 | 1 | 1 | 1 | 1 | 1 | 1 | 1 | 1 | 1 |
| 1 | 1 | 1 | 1 | 1 | 1 | 1 | 1 | 1 | 1 | 1 | 1 | 1 | 1 | 1 | 1 |

| $x$ | $x$ | $x$ | $x$ |
|---|---|---|---|
| $x$ | $x$ | $x$ | $x$ |
| $x$ | $x$ | $x$ | $x$ |
| $x$ | $x$ | $x$ | $x$ |

| $x^2$ | $x^2$ | $x^2$ | $x^2$ |
|---|---|---|---|
| $x^2$ | $x^2$ | $x^2$ | $x^2$ |
| $-x^2$ | $-x^2$ | $-x^2$ | $-x^2$ |
| $-x^2$ | $-x^2$ | $-x^2$ | $-x^2$ |

**Holt Middle School Math    Course 2**

# Are You Ready? Recording Sheet
## Number Theory and Algebraic Reasoning

Choose the best term from the list to complete each sentence.

division    factor    multiplication    place value    product    quotient

1. The operation that gives the quotient of two numbers is _____division_____.
2. The ___place value___ of the digit 3 in 4,903,672 is thousands.
3. A number that is multiplied by another number is called a _____factor_____.
4. The operation that gives the product of two numbers is ___multiplication___.
5. In the equation $15 \div 3 = 5$, the ___quotient___ is 5.

Give the place value of the digit 4 in each number.

| 6. 4,092 | 7. 608,241 | 8. 7,040,000 | 9. 4,556,890,100 |
|---|---|---|---|
| thousands | tens | ten thousands | billions |

| 10. 3,408,289 | 11. 34,506,123 | 12. 500,986,402 | 13. 3,540,277,009 |
|---|---|---|---|
| hundred thousands | millions | hundreds | ten millions |

Find each product.

| 14. $2 \cdot 2 \cdot 2$ | 15. $9 \cdot 9 \cdot 9 \cdot 9$ | 16. $14 \cdot 14 \cdot 14$ | 17. $10 \cdot 10 \cdot 10 \cdot 10$ |
|---|---|---|---|
| 8 | 6,561 | 2,744 | 10,000 |

| 18. $3 \cdot 3 \cdot 5 \cdot 5$ | 19. $2 \cdot 2 \cdot 5 \cdot 7$ | 20. $3 \cdot 3 \cdot 11 \cdot 11$ | 21. $5 \cdot 10 \cdot 10 \cdot 10$ |
|---|---|---|---|
| 225 | 140 | 7,623 | 5,000 |

Find the first five multiples of each number.

22. 2 _____2, 4, 6, 8, 10_____
23. 9 _____9, 18, 27, 36, 45_____
24. 15 _____15, 30, 45, 60, 75_____
25. 1 _____1, 2, 3, 4, 5_____
26. 101 _____101, 202, 303, 404, 506_____
27. 54 _____54, 108, 162, 216, 270_____
28. 326 _____326, 652, 978, 1,304, 1,630_____
29. 1,024 _____1,024, 2,048, 3,072, 4,096, 5,120_____

Holt Middle School Math   Course 2

---

# Are You Ready? Recording Sheet (continued)
## Number Theory and Algebraic Reasoning

List all the factors of each number.

30. 8 _____1, 2, 4, 8_____
31. 22 _____1, 2, 11, 22_____
32. 36 _____1, 2, 3, 4, 6, 9, 12, 18, 36_____
33. 50 _____1, 2, 5, 10, 25, 50_____
34. 108 _____1, 2, 3, 4, 6, 9, 12, 18, 27, 36, 54, 108_____
35. 84 _____1, 2, 3, 4, 6, 7, 12, 14, 21, 28, 42, 84_____
36. 256 _____1, 2, 4, 8, 16, 64, 128, 256_____
37. 630 _____1, 2, 3, 5, 6, 7, 9, 10, 14, 15, 18, 21, 30, 35, 42, 45, 63, 70, 90, 105, 126, 210, 315, 630_____

Holt Middle School Math   Course 2

---

# Exploration Recording Sheet
## Exponents

You can multiply $5 \cdot 5 \cdot 5 \cdot 5 \cdot 5 \cdot 5$ using exponents and a calculator. The number 5 is a factor 6 times, so you can write $5 \cdot 5 \cdot 5 \cdot 5 \cdot 5 \cdot 5$ as $5^6$.
The expressions are equivalent because they have the same value.

| 5•5•5•5•5 | 15625 |
| 5^6 | 15625 |

$$5 \cdot 5 \cdot 5 \cdot 5 \cdot 5 \cdot 5 = 15{,}625 \text{ and } 5^6 = 15{,}625$$

Guess the missing exponent in each statement. Use a calculator after each guess to check your answer.

1. $3^{\square} = 729$ _____6_____
2. $2^{\square} = 4{,}096$ _____12_____
3. $9^{\square} = 4{,}782{,}969$ _____7_____
4. $4^{\square} = 1{,}024$ _____5_____

Number of guesses will vary.

### Think and Discuss

5. **Describe** the strategies you used to find the missing exponents.

   Possible answer: Adjust the exponent up when the power should be greater; adjust the exponent down when the power should be lesser.

6. **Explain** how you can find the value of $2^{11}$ if you know that $2^{10} = 1{,}024$.

   Possible answer: Multiply 1,024 by 2.

Holt Middle School Math

---

# Practice A
## Exponents

Multiply.

1. $4^2$     2. $2^3$     3. $6^2$

$4 \cdot 4 =$ ___16___     $2 \cdot 2 \cdot 2 =$ ___8___     $6 \cdot 6 =$ ___36___

4. $9^2$     5. $4^3$     6. $3^5$     7. $7^0$

___81___     ___64___     ___243___     ___1___

8. $10^2$     9. $3^4$     10. $9^1$     11. $2^5$

___100___     ___81___     ___9___     ___32___

Use an exponent and the given base to write each number.

12. 25, base 5     13. 3, base 3     14. 8, base 2     15. 1, base 4

___$5^2$___     ___$3^1$___     ___$2^3$___     ___$4^0$___

16. 81, base 9     17. 64, base 4     18. 64, base 8     19. 9, base 3

___$9^2$___     ___$4^3$___     ___$8^2$___     ___$3^2$___

20. 36, base 6     21. 16, base 2     22. 27, base 3     23. 400, base 20

___$6^2$___     ___$2^4$___     ___$3^3$___     ___$20^2$___

24. The first day, Jessie has $2. The second day, she has twice as much money as the first day. The third day, she has twice as much money as the second day. Write the amount of money she has on the third day in exponential form. Then write the amount in standard form.

   $2^3$; $8

25. Kevin runs 5 miles on Monday. The total number of miles he runs that week is 5 times the number of miles he runs on Monday. How many miles does Kevin run that week?

   25 miles

Holt Middle School Math   Course 2

---

Holt Middle School Math   Course 2

## Practice B
### Exponents

Find each value.

1. $5^2$    **25**

2. $2^4$    **16**

3. $3^3$    **27**

4. $7^2$    **49**

5. $4^4$    **256**

6. $12^2$    **144**

7. $10^3$    **1,000**

8. $11^1$    **11**

9. $1^6$    **1**

10. $20^2$    **400**

11. $6^3$    **216**

12. $7^3$    **343**

Write each number using an exponent and the given base.

13. 16, base 4    $4^2$

14. 25, base 25    $25^1$

15. 100, base 10    $10^2$

16. 125, base 5    $5^3$

17. 32, base 2    $2^5$

18. 243, base 3    $3^5$

19. 900, base 30    $30^2$

20. 121, base 11    $11^2$

21. 3,600, base 60    $60^2$

22. 256, base 4    $4^4$

23. 512, base 8    $8^3$

24. 196, base 14    $14^2$

25. Damon has 4 times as many stamps as Julia. Julia has 4 times as many stamps as Claire. Claire has 4 stamps. Write the number of stamps Damon has in both exponential form and standard form.

**$4^3$ stamps; 64 stamps**

26. Holly starts a jump rope exercise program. She jumps rope for 3 minutes the first week. In the second week, she triples the time she jumps. In the third week, she triples the time of the second week, and in the fourth week, she triples the time of the third week. How many minutes does she jump rope during the fourth week?

**81 minutes**

   **Holt Middle School Math**   Course 2

---

## Practice C
### Exponents

Find each value.

1. $3^8$    **6,561**

2. $7^5$    **16,807**

3. $50^2$    **2,500**

4. $2^3 + 7^2$    **57**

5. $4^2 + 5^3$    **141**

6. $6^1 + 8^2$    **70**

7. $15^0 + 13^2$    **170**

8. $5^3 - 10^2$    **25**

9. $10^3 - 12^2$    **856**

10. $2^4 + 3^3 - 1^5$    **42**

11. $4^3 - 6^2 + 9^2$    **109**

12. $4^0 + 11^2 - 7^0$    **121**

Write each number using an exponent and the given base.

13. 343, base 7    $7^3$

14. 625, base 5    $5^4$

15. 1,728, base 12    $12^3$

16. 225, base 15    $15^2$

17. 1,000,000, base 100    $100^3$

18. 1,225, base 35    $35^2$

19. 6,561, base 9    $9^4$

20. 2,187, base 3    $3^7$

21. 8,000, base 20    $20^3$

22. Jacob has 7 times as many postcards as Austin has. Austin has 7 times as many postcards as Angela has. Angela has 7 times as many postcards as Samuel has. Samuel has 7 postcards. Write the number of postcards Jacob has in both exponential form and standard form.

**$7^4$ postcards; 2,401 postcards**

   **Holt Middle School Math**   Course 2

---

## Reteach
### Exponents

The exponent tells you how many times to multiply the base by itself.

base $\longrightarrow 3^4 \longleftarrow$ exponent

- To find $3^4$, multiply the base (3) times itself 4 times.

$3^4 = 3 \cdot 3 \cdot 3 \cdot 3 = 81$

> To multiply, say to yourself:
> 3 times 3 is 9
> 9 times 3 is 27
> 27 times 3 is 81

Find each value.

1. $4^3 = $ **4** $\cdot$ **4** $\cdot$ **4** $= 64$

2. $1^5 = $ **1** $\cdot$ **1** $\cdot$ **1** $\cdot$ **1** $\cdot$ **1** $= $ **1**

3. $5^2$   **25**

4. $2^3$   **8**

5. $3^3$   **27**

6. $6^2$   **36**

7. $8^2$   **64**

8. $4^1$   **4**

9. $5^3$   **125**

10. $2^4$   **16**

- You can write 64 using an exponent with the base 8.

> Think: How many times must you multiply 8 times itself to get a product of 64?

$8 \cdot 8 = 64$
So, $64 = 8^2$.

Write each number using an exponent and the given base.

11. 216, base 6: = **36 • 6** and 36 • 6 = **216** so, 216 = **$6^3$**.

12. 16, base 4   $4^2$

13. 8, base 2   $2^3$

14. 9, base 3   $3^2$

15. 81, base 9   $9^2$

16. 27, base 3   $3^3$

17. 49, base 7   $7^2$

   **Holt Middle School Math**   Course 2

---

## Challenge
### Money Grows

If an investment of $50 doubles in value, your investment will be worth $50 • 2 = $100.

If it doubles again, your investment will be worth $50 • 2 • 2 = $200. You can also write this as $50 • $2^2$ = $200.

If your money doubles a third time, it will be worth $50 • $2^3$ = $400.

**Write the correct answer.**

1. If you invest $400, how much will it be worth if it doubles in value twice?    **$1,600**

2. If an investment of $550 doubles in value twice, how much will it be worth?    **$2,200**

3. If you invest $75, how much will it be worth if it doubles in value 4 times?    **$1,200**

4. If you invest $125, how much will it be worth if it doubles in value 4 times?    **$2,000**

5. If an investment of $75 triples in value 3 times, how much will it be worth?    **$2,025**

6. If an investment of $125 triples in value 4 times, how much will it be worth?    **$10,125**

When Jasmine turned 13, she started saving $5 per month until she turned 18. She then invested her total savings so that it doubled in value every 7 years.

7. How much money did Jasmine save by the time she turned 18?   **$300**

8. How many times will her investment double from age 18 to age 60?   **6 times**

9. How much will Jasmine's investment be worth when she turns 60?   **$19,200**

When Jake turned 13, he started saving $1.50 per week until he turned 19. He then invested his total savings so that it tripled in value every 12 years.

10. How much money did Jake save by the time he turned 19?   **$468**

11. How many times will his investment triple from age 19 to age 55?   **3 times**

12. How much will Jake's investment be worth when he turns 55?   **$12,636**

   **Holt Middle School Math**   Course 2

---

   **Holt Middle School Math**   Course 2

## Problem Solving
### 2-1 Exponents

**Write the correct answer.**

**1.** The cells of the bacteria *E. coli* can double every 20 minutes. If you begin with a single cell, how many cells can there be after 4 hours?

**4,096 cells**

**2.** The population of metropolitan Orlando, Florida, has doubled about every 16 years since 1960. In 2000, the population was 1,644,561. At this doubling rate, what could the population be in 2048?

**13,156,488**

**3.** A prizewinner can choose Prize A, $2,000 per year for 15 years, or Prize B, 3 cents the first year, with the amount tripling each year through the fifteenth year. Which prize is more valuable? How much is it worth?

**Prize B: $143,489.07**

**4.** Maria had triplets. Each of her 3 children had triplets. If the pattern continued for 2 more generations, how many great-great-grandchildren would Maria have?

**81 great-great-grandchildren**

**Choose the letter for the best answer.**

**5.** A theory states that the CPU clock speed in a computer doubles every 18 months. If the clock speed was 33 MHz in 1991, how can you use exponents to find out how fast the clock speed is after doubling 3 times?

A $33^3$  
B $3^2 \cdot 33$  
Ⓒ $2^3 \cdot 33$  
D $33^2$

**6.** The classroom is a square with a side length of 13 feet and an area of 169 square feet. How can you write the area in exponential form?

F $2^{13}$  
Ⓖ $13^2$  
H $3^{13}$  
J $13^3$

**7.** In 2000, Wake County, North Carolina, had a population of 610,284. This is about twice the population in 1980. If the county grows at the same rate every 20 years, what will its population be in 2040?

A 915,426  
B 1,220,568  
C 1,830,852  
Ⓓ 2,441,136

**8.** The number of cells of a certain type of bacteria doubles every 45 minutes. If you begin with a single cell, how many cells could there be after 6 hours?

F 64  
Ⓖ 256  
H 360  
J 540

14 Holt Middle School Math Course 2

---

## Puzzles, Twisters & Teasers
### 2-1 Explore Your Power Base!

*Why was the computer tired when it got home?*

To find out, solve each problem. Write the letter on the line above the correct answer at the bottom of the page. Each answer must match exactly. Some letters will not be used.

E    $3^4 =$ **81**

T    49, base 7 = **$7^2$**

K    $10^3 =$ **1,000**

B    81, base 9 = **$9^2$**

I    $2^6 =$ **64**

D    $5^2 =$ **25**

W    $18^1 =$ **18**

C    25, base 5 = **$5^2$**

A    27, base 3 = **$3^3$**

H    $14^0 =$ **1**

V    $12^2 =$ **144**

R    256, base 4 = **$4^4$**

O    216, base 6 = **$6^3$**

U    $5^3 =$ **125**

S    $6^2 =$ **36**

$$\underset{9^2}{B}\ \underset{81}{E}\ \underset{5^2}{C}\ \underset{3^3}{A}\ \underset{125}{U}\ \underset{36}{S}\ \underset{81}{E}\ \underset{64}{I}\ \underset{7^2}{T}\ \underset{1}{H}\ \underset{3^3}{A}\ \underset{25}{D}$$

$$\underset{3^3}{A}\ \underset{1}{H}\ \underset{3^3}{A}\ \underset{4^4}{R}\ \underset{25}{D}\ \underset{25}{D}\ \underset{4^4}{R}\ \underset{64}{I}\ \underset{144}{V}\ \underset{81}{E}$$

15 Holt Middle School Math Course 2

---

## Exploration Recording Sheet
### 2-2 Powers of Ten and Scientific Notation

**1.** Complete the table and look for a pattern.

| Power of 10 | Factors | Product |
|---|---|---|
| $10^1$ | 10 | 10 |
| $10^2$ | $10 \cdot 10$ | 100 |
| $10^3$ | $10 \cdot 10 \cdot 10$ | 1,000 |
| $10^4$ | $10 \cdot 10 \cdot 10 \cdot 10$ | 10,000 |
| $10^5$ | $10 \cdot 10 \cdot 10 \cdot 10 \cdot 10$ | 100,000 |
| $10^6$ | $10 \cdot 10 \cdot 10 \cdot 10 \cdot 10 \cdot 10$ | 1,000,000 |
| $10^9$ | $10 \cdot 10 \cdot 10 \cdot 10 \cdot 10 \cdot 10 \cdot 10 \cdot 10 \cdot 10$ | 1,000,000,000 |

**2.** Use the pattern you observed in the table to write 10,000,000 as a power of 10.

**$10^7$**

**Think and Discuss**

**3. Describe** the pattern you observed in the table.

**Possible answer: The exponent of 10 equal to the number of zeros after 1 in the product.**

**4. Explain** how you know that $100,000 = 10^5$ is a true statement.

**Possible answer: The number of zeros after 1 and the exponent are both 5.**

17 Holt Middle School Math Course 2

---

## Practice A
### 2-2 Powers of Ten and Scientific Notation

**Choose the letter for the best answer.**

**1.** $4 \cdot 10^2$  
A 4  
B 40  
Ⓒ 400  
D 100

**2.** $16 \cdot 10^0$  
F 1600  
Ⓖ 16  
H 10  
J 0

**3.** $9 \cdot 10^3$  
Ⓐ 9,000  
B 900  
C 90  
D 9

**4.** $17 \cdot 10^1$  
F 1.7  
G 17  
Ⓗ 170  
J 1700

**Multiply.**

**5.** $23 \cdot 10^2$   **2,300**

**6.** $15 \cdot 10^4$   **150,000**

**7.** $30 \cdot 10^2$   **3,000**

**8.** $28 \cdot 10^3$   **28,000**

**9.** $132 \cdot 10^2$   **13,200**

**10.** $201 \cdot 10^3$   **201,000**

**11.** $456 \cdot 10^2$   **45,600**

**12.** $108 \cdot 10^4$   **1,080,000**

**Write the number in scientific notation.**

**13.** 56,000   **$5.6 \times 10^4$**

**14.** 306,000   **$3.06 \times 10^5$**

**15.** 8,000,000   **$8.0 \times 10^6$**

**16.** 7,200,000   **$7.2 \times 10^6$**

**17.** 14,000,000   **$1.4 \times 10^7$**

**18.** 41.00   **$4.1 \times 10^1$**

**19.** 2,144,000   **$2.144 \times 10^6$**

**20.** $20.3 \cdot 10^5$   **$2.03 \times 10^6$**

**21.** Lake Huron covers an area of about 23,000 square miles. Write this number in scientific notation.

**$2.3 \times 10^4$**

**22.** The planet Mercury is about $3.6 \times 10^7$ miles from the sun. Write this number in standard form.

**36,000,000**

18 Holt Middle School Math Course 2

---

## Practice B
### Powers of Ten and Scientific Notation

**Multiply.**

1. $6 \cdot 10^3$
6,000

2. $22 \cdot 10^1$
220

3. $8 \cdot 10^2$
800

4. $18 \cdot 10^0$
18

5. $70 \cdot 10^2$
7,000

6. $25 \cdot 10^3$
25,000

7. $3 \cdot 10^4$
30,000

8. $180 \cdot 10^3$
180,000

**Find each product.**

9. $84 \cdot 10^4$
840,000

10. $315 \cdot 10^2$
31,500

11. $210 \cdot 10^3$
210,000

12. $1,004 \cdot 10^3$
1,004,000

13. $1,764 \cdot 10^1$
17,640

14. $856 \cdot 10^0$
856

15. $4,055 \cdot 10^3$
4,055,000

16. $716 \cdot 10^4$
7,160,000

**Write each number in scientific notation.**

17. 34,000
$3.4 \times 10^4$

18. 7,700
$7.7 \times 10^3$

19. 2,100,000
$2.1 \times 10^6$

20. 404,000
$4.04 \times 10^5$

21. 21,000,000
$2.1 \times 10^7$

22. 612.00
$6.12 \times 10^2$

23. 3,001,000
$3.001 \times 10^6$

24. $62.13 \cdot 10^4$
$6.213 \times 10^5$

25. Lake Superior covers an area of about 31,700 square miles. Write this number in scientific notation.

$3.17 \times 10^4$

26. Mars is about $1.42 \cdot 10^8$ miles from the sun. Write this number in standard form.

142,000,000

27. In 1999, the population of China was about $1.25 \cdot 10^9$. What was the population of China written in standard form?

1,250,000,000

28. A scientist estimates there are 4,800,000 bacteria in a test tube. How does she record the number using scientific notation?

$4.8 \times 10^6$

---

## Practice C
### Powers of Ten and Scientific Notation

**Multiply.**

1. $5 \cdot 10^3$
5,000

2. $471 \cdot 10^2$
47,100

3. $39.5 \cdot 10^1$
395

4. $200 \cdot 10^5$
20,000,000

5. $7,025 \cdot 10^0$
7,025

6. $5.7 \cdot 10^6$
5,700,000

7. $66.25 \cdot 10^4$
662,500

8. $9.01 \cdot 10^9$
9,010,000,000

**Write each number in scientific notation.**

9. 25,000
$2.5 \times 10^4$

10. 9,900
$9.9 \times 10^3$

11. 9,700,000
$9.7 \times 10^6$

12. $95.6 \times 10^8$
$9.56 \times 10^9$

13. 23,000,000,000
$2.3 \times 10^{10}$

14. 110.00
$1.1 \times 10^2$

15. $301.9 \times 10^5$
$3.019 \times 10^7$

16. $73.55 \times 10^4$
$7.355 \times 10^5$

**Write the missing number or numbers.**

17. $1.23 \times 10^? = 12,300$
4

18. $8.3 \times 10^5 = ?$
830,000

19. $112,000,000 = ? \times 10^8$
1.12

20. $410,000 = ? \times 10^5$
4.1

21. $7.7 \times 10^7 = ?$
77,000,000

22. $2,950,000 = 2.95 \times 10^?$
6

23. The Caspian Sea covers an area of about 143,250 square miles. Write this number in scientific notation.

$1.4325 \times 10^5$

24. The distance between Jupiter and Saturn is about $4.03 \times 10^8$ miles. Write this number in standard form.

403,000,000

25. In 1999, the population of the world was about $5.996 \times 10^9$. What was the population in standard form?

5,996,000,000

26. A scientist estimates there are 37,000,000 bacteria in a petri dish. He records the number using scientific notation. What does he write?

$3.7 \times 10^7$

---

## Reteach
### Powers of Ten and Scientific Notation

To multiply by a power of 10, use the exponent to find the number of zeros in the product.

• Multiply $42 \cdot 10^4$.

The exponent 4 tells you to write 4 zeros after 42 in the product.

$42 \cdot 10^4 = 420,000$

**Find each product.**

1. $84 \cdot 10^3$

The product should have __3__ zeros.

$84 \cdot 10^3 = $ __84,000__

2. $61 \cdot 10^5$

The product should have __5__ zeros.

$61 \cdot 10^5 = $ __6,100,000__

3. $22 \cdot 10^6$
22,000,000

4. $753 \cdot 10^3$
753,000

5. $825 \cdot 10^2$
82,500

6. $123 \cdot 10^1$
1,230

• Write 926,000 in scientific notation.

First, write the digits before the zeros as a number greater than or equal to 1 and less than 10. The number must have only 1 digit to the left of the decimal point. That digit cannot be zero.

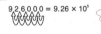

Think: 9.26 is greater than 1 and less than 10.

Then multiply 9.26 by the power of 10 that gives 926,000 as the product.

$9\underset{\curvearrowleft}{2}6{,}0\,0\,0 = 9.26 \times 10^5$

The decimal point moves 5 places so the exponent is 5.

**Write each number in scientific notation.**

7. 5,100

The decimal point moves __3__ places.

$5,100 = $ __5__ . __1__ $\times 10^{\underline{3}}$

8. 1,840,000

The decimal point moves __6__ places.

$1,840,000 = $ __1__ . __84__ $\times 10^{\underline{6}}$

9. 641,000
$6.41 \times 10^5$

10. 47,300
$4.73 \times 10^4$

11. 8,250,000
$8.25 \times 10^6$

12. 703,000
$7.03 \times 10^5$

---

## Challenge
### Computer Bytes

Each byte in a computer's memory represents about one character. The major units of computer memory are kilobytes (KB), megabytes (MB), and gigabytes (GB).

| | |
|---|---|
| 1 kilobyte  = 1,000 bytes | 1 KB = 1,000 bytes |
| 1 megabyte = 1,000 kilobytes | 1 MG = 1,000 KB |
| 1 gigabyte  = 1,000 megabytes | 1 GB = 1,000 MB |

**Write your answers using scientific notation.**

1. In 1984, many personal computers had 64 KB of active (RAM) memory. How many bytes does this represent?

$6.4 \times 10^4$ bytes

2. In 1992, many personal computers had 40 MB of hard drive memory. How many bytes does this represent?

$4 \times 10^7$ bytes

3. In 1997, many personal computers had 1 GB of hard drive memory. How many bytes does this represent?

$1 \times 10^9$ bytes

4. By 2001, many personal computers had 20 GB of hard drive memory. How many bytes does this represent?

$2 \times 10^{10}$ bytes

Ming saved his computer files on floppy disks. Each disk holds up to 1.44 MB of memory. He used these disks to transfer his files to another computer.

5. How many bytes could each floppy disk hold?

$1.44 \times 10^6$ bytes

6. Ming's new computer has 12 GB of memory. How many disks could he transfer if each disk held 1.2 MB?

10,000 disks

Rachel decided to back up her hard drive's computer files by copying them onto compact disks (CDs). Each CD can hold up to 650 MB of memory, but Rachel saves only 600 MB on each.

7. How many bytes could each CD potentially hold?

$6.5 \times 10^8$ bytes

8. If Rachel backs up 6 GB of memory, how many bytes of memory will she need?

$6 \times 10^9$ bytes

---

## LESSON 2-2 Problem Solving
### Powers of Ten and Scientific Notation

**Write the correct answer.**

1. Earth is about 150,000,000 kilometers from the sun. Write this distance in scientific notation.

   $1.5 \times 10^8$ km

2. The planet Neptune is about $4.5 \times 10^9$ kilometers from the sun. Write this distance in standard form.

   4,500,000,000 km

3. In 1999, the U.S. federal debt was about $5 trillion, 600 billion. Write the amount of the debt in standard form and in scientific notation.

   \$5,600,000,000,000;

   $5.6 \times 10^{12}$

4. Canada is about $1.0 \times 10^7$ square kilometers in size. Brazil is about 8,500,000 square kilometers in size. Which country has a greater area?

   Canada

**Choose the letter for the best answer.**

5. China's population in 2001 was approximately 1,273,000,000. Mexico's population for the same year was about $1.02 \times 10^8$. How much greater was China's population than Mexico's?
   A 1,375,000,000
   B 1,274,020,000
   Ⓒ 1,171,000,000
   D 102,000,000

6. In mid-2001, the world population was approximately $6.137 \times 10^9$. By 2050, the population is projected to be $9.036 \times 10^9$. By how much will world population increase?
   F 151,730,000
   G 289,900,000
   H 1,517,300,000
   Ⓙ 2,899,000,000

7. The Alpha Centauri star system is about 4.3 light-years from Earth. One light-year, the distance light travels in 1 year, is about 6 trillion miles. About how many miles away from Earth is Alpha Centauri?
   Ⓐ $2.58 \times 10^{13}$ miles
   B $6 \times 10^{13}$ miles
   C $1.03 \times 10^{12}$ miles
   D $2.58 \times 10^9$ miles

8. In the fall of 2001, students in Columbia, South Carolina, raised \$440,000 to buy a new fire truck for New York City. If the money had been collected in pennies, how many pennies would that have been?
   F $4.4 \times 10^6$
   G $4.4 \times 10^5$
   Ⓗ $4.4 \times 10^7$
   J 4.4 3 $10^8$

Holt Middle School Math   Course 2

---

## LESSON 2-2 Puzzles, Twisters & Teasers
### Oh, the Power of Tens!

Substitute the correct number for the letter or letters in each equation. Use your answers to solve the riddle.

1. $24{,}500 = 2.45 \times 10^E$   ___4___
2. $280{,}000 = 2.8 \times 10^P$   ___5___
3. $592{,}000 = I \times 10^5$   ___5.92___
4. $16{,}800 = C \times 10^4$   ___1.68___
5. $5.4 \times 10^H = 540{,}000{,}000$   ___8___
6. $24{,}400{,}000 = S \times 10^A$   ___7___

What's a Martian's favorite snack?

| S | P | A | C | E | C | H | I | P | S |
|---|---|---|---|---|---|---|---|---|---|
| 2.44 | 5 | 7 | 1.68 | 4 | 1.68 | 8 | 5.92 | 5 | 2.44 |

Holt Middle School Math   Course 2

---

## LESSON 2-3 Exploration Recording Sheet
### Order of Operations

Many calculators are programmed to compute in a certain order, called the *order of operations.*

1. Determine the order the calculator follows for each expression in the window.

In $5 + 2 \times 3$ the calculator performs $2 \times 3$ first, then adds 5. In $(5 + 2) \times 3$, the calculator performs the addition $5 + 2$, then multiplies by 3.

Use the necessary operation symbols $+$, $-$, $\times$, and $\div$ and the grouping symbols $)$ and $($ to make each statement true. Verify with your calculator.

2. $4 \; 3 \; 6 = 7$   $4 - 3 + 6 = 7$
3. $4 \; 3 \; 6 = 6$   $(4 - 3) \times 6 \text{ or } 4 \times 3 - 6$
4. $4 \; 3 \; 6 = 22$   $4 + (3 \times 6)$
5. $4 \; 3 \; 6 = 42$   $(4 + 3) \times 6$
6. $4 \; 3 \; 6 = 2$   $4 \times (3 \div 6)$
7. $6 \; 3 \; 4 = 8$   $(6 \div 3) \times 4$

**Think and Discuss**

8. **Explain** how the grouping symbols $)$ and $($ are used in the order of operations.

   Possible answer: Grouping symbols are used to indicate operations that are to be performed first.

9. **Describe** the order of operations in your own words.

   Possible answer: Grouped operations, exponents, multiplication and division from left to right and then addition and subtraction from left to right.

Holt Middle School Math   Course 2

---

## LESSON 2-3 Practice A
### Order of Operations

**Choose the letter for the best answer.**

1. $75 + 12 \cdot 2$
   A 87
   Ⓑ 99
   C 108
   D 174

2. $100 - 25 \div 5$
   F 15
   G 75
   H 80
   Ⓙ 95

3. $50 - 18 \div 6 + 2$
   Ⓐ 49
   B 40
   C 10
   D 4

4. $72 - 4^2 \cdot 2$
   F 32
   Ⓖ 40
   H 56
   J 64

5. $(8 + 22) \div 5 + 5$
   A 30
   B 17.4
   Ⓒ 11
   D 3

6. $3^3 - (9 \cdot 2 + 1)$
   F 19
   G 10
   Ⓗ 8
   J −10

**Evaluate.**

7. $2^4 \div 8 + 5$

   7

8. $18 + 2(1 + 3^2)$

   38

9. $(16 \div 4) + 4 \cdot (2^2 - 2)$

   12

10. $2^3 - (3 \cdot 5 - 8)$

    1

11. $35 + 4^2 - (6 - 3)$

    48

12. $6 \cdot 7 - 3(4 + 1)$

    27

13. $100 \div 5 \cdot 2^2$

    80

14. $(5 + 2)^2 \div 7 - 6$

    1

15. $15 - 3 \cdot 4 \div 2 + 5$

    14

16. Leon rents a video game for \$5. He returns the video game 3 days late. The late fee is \$1 for each day late. Evaluate the expression $5 + 3 \cdot 1$ to find out how much it costs Leon to rent the video game.

    \$8

17. Olivia shovels snow for 6 neighbors. Each neighbor pays her \$8. Two neighbors each give her a \$2 tip as well. Evaluate $6 \cdot 8 + 2 \cdot 2$ to find out how much money Olivia earns in all.

    \$52

Holt Middle School Math   Course 2

---

Holt Middle School Math   Course 2

**Evaluate.**

**1.** $15 \cdot 3 + 12 \cdot 2$
    69

**2.** $212 + 21 \div 3$
    219

**3.** $9 \cdot 3 - 18 \div 3$
    21

**4.** $65 - 36 \div 3$
    53

**5.** $100 - 9^2 + 2$
    21

**6.** $3 \cdot 5 - 45 \div 3^2$
    10

**7.** $54 \div 6 + 4 \cdot 6$
    33

**8.** $(6 + 5) \cdot 16 \div 2$
    88

**9.** $60 - 8 \cdot 12 \div 3$
    28

**10.** $45 - 3^2 \cdot 5$
    0

**11.** $52 - (8 \cdot 2 \div 4) + 3^2$
    57

**12.** $(2^3 + 10 \div 2) \cdot 3$
    39

**13.** $25 + 7(18 - 4^2)$
    39

**14.** $(6 \cdot 3 - 12)^2 \div 9 + 7$
    11

**15.** $4^3 - (3 + 12 \cdot 2 - 9)$
    46

**16.** $2^4 + 8 + 5$
    7

**17.** $(1 + 2)^2 \cdot (3 - 1)^2 \div 2$
    18

**18.** $(16 \div 4) + 4 \cdot (2^2 - 2)$
    12

**19.** $2^5 - (3 \cdot 7 - 7)$
    18

**20.** $75 + 5^2 - (8 - 3)$
    95

**21.** $9 \cdot 6 - 5(10 - 3)$
    19

**22.** $96 \div 4 + 5 \cdot 2^2$
    44

**23.** $(15 - 6)^2 \div 3 - 3^3$
    0

**24.** $19 - 8 \cdot 5 \div 10 + 6 \div 3$
    17

**25.** Jared has $32. He buys 5 packs of trading cards that cost
$3 each and a display book that costs $7. Evaluate
$32 - (5 \cdot 3 + 7)$ to find out how much money Jared has left.

$10

**26.** David buys 3 movie tickets for $6 each and 2 bags of popcorn
for $2 each. Evaluate $3 \cdot 6 + 2 \cdot 2$ to find out how much money
David spent in all.

$22

 **Holt Middle School Math   Course 2**

---

**Evaluate.**

**1.** $25 \cdot 3 + 60 \cdot 2$
    195

**2.** $350 \div 5 + 12 \cdot 7$
    154

**3.** $3 \cdot 9 + 96 \div 4$
    51

**4.** $77 - 42 \div 7^1$
    71

**5.** $532 - 2^5 \div 4$
    524

**6.** $3(20 - 4^2) + 7$
    19

**7.** $270 \div 6 + 6^2$
    81

**8.** $(5 + 6)^2 + 18 \div 2$
    130

**9.** $10^2 - 25 \cdot 3 \div 5$
    85

**10.** $65 - 4^3 \cdot 1^7$
    1

**11.** $40 - (5 \cdot 2) + 8$
    38

**12.** $(6^2 + 4) \div 5$
    8

**13.** $2^4 \div 8 + 5$
    7

**14.** $(1 + 2)^2 \cdot (3 - 1)^2 \div 2$
    18

**15.** $(16 \div 4) + 4 \cdot (2^2 - 2)$
    12

**Insert grouping symbols to make a true statement.**

**16.** $18 + 2 \cdot 1 + 3^2 = 38$
    $18 + 2(1 + 3^2)$

**17.** $4 \cdot 2 - 2^2 \div 9 + 2 = 6$
    $(4 \cdot 2 - 2^2) \div 9 + 2$

**18.** $3^3 - 9 \cdot 2 + 1 = 8$
    $3^3 - (9 \cdot 2 + 1)$

**19.** $2^3 - 3 \cdot 5 - 8 = 1$
    $2^3 - (3 \cdot 5 - 8)$

**20.** $35 + 4^2 - 6 - 3 = 48$
    $35 + 4^2 - (6 - 3)$

**21.** $6 \cdot 7 - 3 \cdot 4 + 1 = 27$
    $6 \cdot 7 - 3 \cdot (4 + 1)$

**22.** A group of students charges $7 to clean the exterior and $6 to
clean the interior of a car. They clean 9 exteriors and 5 interiors.
Evaluate $7 \cdot 9 + 6 \cdot 5$ to find out how much money the students
raised in all.

$93

**23.** Ariel has $65. She buys 5 books that cost $8.00 each, a
bookmark that costs $2.00, and a magazine that costs $4.00.
Evaluate $65 - (5 \cdot 8 + 2 + 4)$ to find out how much money Ariel
has left.

$19

 **Holt Middle School Math   Course 2**

---

To help you remember the order of operations use the phrase
"**P**lease **E**xcuse **M**y **D**ear **A**unt **S**ally."

> **P**: first, **p**arentheses (if any)
> **E**: second, **e**xponents (if any)
> **M** and **D**: then, **m**ultiplication and **d**ivision, in order from left to right
> **A** and **S**: finally, **a**ddition and **s**ubtraction, in order from left to right

Evaluate.                              $39 \div (9 + 4) + 5 - 2^2$
            Parentheses $\longrightarrow$ $39 \div 13 + 5 - 2^2$
            Exponents $\longrightarrow$ $39 \div 13 + 5 - 4$
Multiply and divide from left to right $\longrightarrow$ $3 + 5 - 4$
Add and subtract from left to right $\longrightarrow$ $8 - 4 = 4$

**Evaluate.**

**1.** $12 \cdot 4 - 2$
    48 $- 2$
    46

**2.** $15 \div 3 \cdot 5$
    5 $\cdot 5$
    25

**3.** $15 \cdot 3 \div 5$
    45 $\div 5$
    9

**4.** $8 + 20 \div 4$
    13

**5.** $5 - 2 \cdot 6 \div 4 + 1$
    3

**6.** $3^2 + 6 \cdot 4 - 5^2$
    8

**7.** $1 + 4 \cdot 9 \div 6 - 7$
    0

**8.** $18 \div (6 \div 3)$
    9

**9.** $(18 \div 6) \div 3$
    1

**10.** $4 \cdot 5 + 8 \div 2 - 7$
    17

**11.** $2 \cdot 3 - 8 \div 2^2$
    4

**12.** $8(7 - 6) \div 2^3$
    1

 **Holt Middle School Math   Course 2**

---

A *fixed cost* is a one-time cost. A *variable cost* changes depending
on your use of a product or a service.

The annual enrollment fee per year at a fitness club (fixed cost) is
$30. You also pay $2 per visit (variable cost), and you visit the club
8 times per month. What is your total annual cost?

    $2 \cdot (8 \cdot 12)$       variable cost times total visits
    $30 + 2 \cdot (8 \cdot 12)$       total annual cost
    222       Your total annual cost is $222.

**Use the information above to solve problems 1–4.**

**1.** Suppose the annual fee is $25, but
the cost per visit is $3. What is your
annual cost?

$313

**2.** Suppose you visit the club 3 times
per week instead of 8 times per
month. What is your annual cost?

$342

**3.** Suppose the cost per visit is $3 after
the first 50 visits per year. What is
your annual cost?

$268

**4.** Suppose you pay for up to 75 visits
per year. Any additional visits are
free. What is your annual cost?

$180

The school band is raising money for a trip. The members ordered
5 dozen jerseys for $7 each and sold them for $12 each. They also
ordered 4 dozen sweatshirts for $11 each and sold them for $18
each. The band paid $35 to create the design.

**5.** Write and evaluate an expression to calculate the band's
variable costs for the clothing.

$7(5 \cdot 12) + 11(4 \cdot 12)$; $948

**6.** Write and evaluate an expression to calculate the band's total
cost, including fixed costs.

$7(5 \cdot 12) + 11(4 \cdot 12) + 35$; $983

**7.** Write and evaluate an expression to calculate the band's profit.

$12(5 \cdot 12) + 18(4 \cdot 12) - [7(5 \cdot 12) + 11(4 \cdot 12) + 35]$; $601

**8.** What would the profit be if jerseys sold for $10 and sweatshirts
sold for $20?

$577

 **Holt Middle School Math   Course 2**

---

**135** **Holt Middle School Math   Course 2**

Write the correct answer.

1. In 1975, the minimum wage was $2.10 per hour. Write and evaluate an expression to show wages earned in a 35-hour week after a $12 tax deduction.

$35 \cdot 2.10 - 12; \$61.50$

2. George bought 3 boxes of Girl Scout cookies at $3.50 per box and 4 boxes at $3.00 per box. Write and evaluate an expression to show his total cost.

$3 \cdot 3.50 + 4 \cdot 3; \$22.50$

3. In 1 week Ed works 4 days, 3 hours a day, for $12 per hour, and 2 days, 6 hours a day, for $15 per hour. Evaluate $12(4 \cdot 3) + 15(2 \cdot 6)$ to find Ed's weekly earnings.

$324 per week

4. Keisha had $150. She bought jeans for $27, a sweater for $32, 3 blouses for $16 each, and 2 pairs of socks for $6 each. Evaluate $150 - [27 + 32 + (3 \cdot 16) + (2 \cdot 6)]$ to find out how much money she has left.

She has $31 left.

Choose the letter for the best answer.

5. As of September 1, 1997, the minimum wage was $5.15 per hour. How much more would someone earn now than in 1997 if she earns $5 more per hour for a 40-hour week?
   A $206 more
   **B** $200 more
   C $406 more
   D $400 more

6. Gary received $200 in birthday gifts. He bought 5 CDs for $15 each, 2 posters for $12 each, and a $70 jacket. How much money does he have left?
   **F** $31
   G $10
   H $132
   J $169

7. Yvonne took her younger brother and his friends to the movies. She bought 5 tickets for $8 each, 4 drinks for $2 each, and two $3 containers of popcorn. How much did she spend?
   A $22
   B $51
   **C** $54
   D $38

8. On a business trip, Mr. Chang stayed in a hotel for 7 nights. He paid $149 per night. While he was there, he made 8 phone calls at $2 each and charged $81 to room service. How much did he spend?
   F $246
   G $946
   H $1,043
   **J** $1,140

---

*What's the last thing you take off before you go to bed?*

Decide whether each statement below is true or false. Use your answers to solve the riddle.

1. A numerical expression is made up of numbers and operations.
   **(T)**    F

2. In mathematics, as in life, tasks may be done in any order.
   T    **(F)**

3. When using the order of operations, you should do division after subtraction.
   T    **(F)**

4. When using the order of operations, you should subtract and add from left to right.
   **(T)**    F

5. When using the order of operations, you should divide and multiply from right to left.
   T    **(F)**

6. When an expression has a set of grouping symbols within a second set of grouping symbols, you should begin with the innermost set.
   **(T)**    F

7. You should perform operations inside parentheses first.
   **(T)**    F

8. When using the order of operations, you should evaluate the exponent expression after multiplying and adding.
   T    **(F)**

9. Mathematicians agree on using the order of operations.
   **(T)**    F

| T |
| L F Y |
| R H |

| F |
| O T |
| E U |

You take $\underset{T}{Y} \underset{F}{O} \underset{F}{U} \underset{T}{R}$  $\underset{T}{F} \underset{F}{E} \underset{F}{E} \underset{F}{T}$  $\underset{F}{O} \underset{T}{F} \underset{T}{F}$

$\underset{F}{T} \underset{T}{H} \underset{F}{E}$  $\underset{T}{F} \underset{T}{L} \underset{F}{O} \underset{F}{O} \underset{T}{R}$.

---

| | | ② | ③ | | ⑤ |
|---|---|---|---|---|---|
| | ⑦ | | | | ⑪ |
| | ⑬ | | | | ⑰ |
| | ⑲ | | | | |
| | | | | | ㉙ |
| | ㉛ | | | | |
| | ㊲ | | | | ㊶ |
| | ㊸ | | | | ㊼ |
| | | | | | ㊿ |

| | | | | | ㉟ |
|---|---|---|---|---|---|
| | ⑥① | | | | |
| | ⑥⑦ | | | | ⑦① |
| | ⑦③ | | | | |
| | ⑦⑨ | | | | ⑧③ |
| | | | | | ⑧⑨ |
| | ⑨① | | | | ⑨⑤ |
| | ⑨⑦ | | | | ⑩① |
| ⑩② | ⑩③ | ⑩④ | ⑩⑤ | ⑩⑥ | ⑩⑦ |

Use the number chart to complete the steps.

1. Circle the number 2. Then cross out all of the multiples of 2.
2. Circle the number 3. Then cross out all of the multiples of 3.
3. Circle the number 5. Then cross out all of the multiples of 5.
4. Circle any number remaining if its only factors are itself and 1, and cross out the others.

**Think and Discuss**

5. **Compare** your chart with others. Do your charts agree? Why or why not?

   Possible answer: Some charts do not agree because 49, 77 and 91 were overlooked.

6. **Describe** some patterns you discovered in the number chart.

   Possible answer: Multiples of 2, 3 and 6 occur in columns.

---

Choose the letter for the best answer.

1. What is the prime factorization of 24?
   **(A)** $2^3 \cdot 3$
   B $3^2 \cdot 2$
   C $2^2 \cdot 3^2$
   D $2^3 \cdot 3^2$

2. What is the prime factorization of 50?
   F $3 \cdot 5^2$
   G $3^2 \cdot 5$
   **(H)** $2 \cdot 5^2$
   J $2^2 \cdot 5^2$

3. What is the prime factorization of 35?
   A $2 \cdot 3 \cdot 5$
   **(B)** $5 \cdot 7$
   C $3^2 \cdot 5$
   D $3^2 \cdot 7$

4. What is the prime factorization of 27?
   **(F)** $3^3$
   G $2^3 \cdot 3^2$
   H $9^2$
   J $2^2 \cdot 3^2$

Use a factor tree to find the prime factorization.

5. 25

   $5^2$

6. 20

   $2^2 \cdot 5$

7. 32

   $2^5$

8. 49

   $7^2$

9. 30

   $2 \cdot 3 \cdot 5$

10. 44

    $2^2 \cdot 11$

11. 63

    $3^2 \cdot 7$

12. 28

    $2^2 \cdot 7$

Use a step diagram to find the prime factorization.

13. 93

    $3 \cdot 31$

14. 110

    $2 \cdot 5 \cdot 11$

15. 80

    $2^4 \cdot 5$

16. 42

    $2 \cdot 3 \cdot 7$

17. 625

    $5^4$

18. 98

    $2 \cdot 7^2$

19. 140

    $2^2 \cdot 5 \cdot 7$

20. 92

    $2^2 \cdot 23$

21. 200

    $2^3 \cdot 5^2$

22. 105

    $3 \cdot 5 \cdot 7$

23. 363

    $3 \cdot 11^2$

24. 252

    $2^2 \cdot 3^2 \cdot 7$

## Practice B
### Prime Factorization

Use a factor tree to find the prime factorization.

**1.** 57
$3 \cdot 19$

**2.** 49
$7^2$

**3.** 88
$2^3 \cdot 11$

**4.** 95
$5 \cdot 19$

**5.** 105
$3 \cdot 5 \cdot 7$

**6.** 98
$2 \cdot 7^2$

**7.** 52
$2^2 \cdot 13$

**8.** 42
$2 \cdot 3 \cdot 7$

**9.** 68
$2^2 \cdot 17$

**10.** 91
$7 \cdot 13$

**11.** 60
$2^2 \cdot 3 \cdot 5$

**12.** 72
$2^3 \cdot 3^2$

**13.** 189
$3^3 \cdot 7$

**14.** 270
$2 \cdot 3^3 \cdot 5$

**15.** 140
$2^2 \cdot 5 \cdot 7$

**16.** 1,323
$3^3 \cdot 7^2$

Use a step diagram to find the prime factorization.

**17.** 56
$2^3 \cdot 7$

**18.** 144
$2^4 \cdot 3^2$

**19.** 370
$2 \cdot 5 \cdot 37$

**20.** 168
$2^3 \cdot 3 \cdot 7$

**21.** 124
$2^2 \cdot 31$

**22.** 515
$5 \cdot 103$

**23.** 725
$5^2 \cdot 29$

**24.** 220
$2^2 \cdot 5 \cdot 11$

**25.** 126
$2 \cdot 3^2 \cdot 7$

**26.** 104
$2^3 \cdot 13$

**27.** 66
$2 \cdot 3 \cdot 11$

**28.** 175
$5^2 \cdot 7$

**29.** 450
$2 \cdot 3^2 \cdot 5^2$

**30.** 1,000
$2^3 \cdot 5^3$

**31.** 1,040
$2^4 \cdot 5 \cdot 13$

**32.** 2,500
$2^2 \cdot 5^4$

**33.** The prime factorization of a number is $3^2 \cdot 5 \cdot 11$. What is the number?
495

---

## Practice C
### Prime Factorization

Use a factor tree to find the prime factorization.

**1.** 84
$2^2 \cdot 3 \cdot 7$

**2.** 343
$7^3$

**3.** 135
$3^3 \cdot 5$

**4.** 180
$2^2 \cdot 3^2 \cdot 5$

**5.** 48
$2^4 \cdot 3$

**6.** 225
$3^2 \cdot 5^2$

**7.** 93
$3 \cdot 31$

**8.** 126
$2 \cdot 3^2 \cdot 7$

Use a step diagram to find the prime factorization.

**9.** 290
$2 \cdot 5 \cdot 29$

**10.** 900
$2^2 \cdot 3^2 \cdot 5^2$

**11.** 575
$5^2 \cdot 23$

**12.** 90
$2 \cdot 3^2 \cdot 5$

**13.** 220
$2^2 \cdot 5 \cdot 11$

**14.** 350
$2 \cdot 5^2 \cdot 7$

**15.** 495
$3^2 \cdot 5 \cdot 11$

**16.** 480
$2^5 \cdot 3 \cdot 5$

**17.** 2,000
$2^4 \cdot 5^3$

**18.** 1,040
$2^4 \cdot 5 \cdot 13$

**19.** 1,650
$2 \cdot 3 \cdot 5^2 \cdot 11$

**20.** 3,000
$2^3 \cdot 3 \cdot 5^3$

**21.** The prime factorization of a number is $2^2 \cdot 3^5$. What is the number?
972

**22.** You can factor 150 as 15 • 10. List four other ways can you factor 150.
$5 \cdot 30; 3 \cdot 50; 6 \cdot 25; 2 \cdot 75$

**23.** A number $x$ is a prime factor of 65 and 104. What is the number?
13

Write the composite number for each prime factorization.

**24.** $2^5 \cdot 5^2$
800

**25.** $3^3 \cdot 5 \cdot 11$
1,485

**26.** $4^3 \cdot 7 \cdot 13$
5,824

**27.** $2^8 \cdot 3^5$
62,208

**28.** The prime factors of a number are all the prime numbers between 20 and 30. No factor is repeated. What is the number?
667

---

## Reteach
### Prime Factorization

To write the **prime factorization** of a number, write the number as the product of only prime numbers. A prime number has only two factors, itself and 1.

Use a *factor tree* to find the prime factorization of 18.

Use a *factor tree* to find the prime factorization of 36.

Keep factoring until all the factors are prime.

The prime factorization of 18 is $2 \cdot 3 \cdot 3$, or $2 \cdot 3^2$.

The prime factorization of 36 is $2 \cdot 2 \cdot 3 \cdot 3$, or $2^2 \cdot 3^2$.

Use a factor tree to find the prime factorization.

**1.** 20
$2^2 \cdot 5$

**2.** 28
$2^2 \cdot 7$

**3.** 54
$2 \cdot 3^3$

**4.** 63
$3^2 \cdot 7$

Use a *step diagram* to find the prime factorization of 60.

$$\begin{array}{r} 2|60 \\ 2|30 \\ 3|15 \\ 5|5 \\ 1 \end{array}$$

1) The divisors must be prime numbers.
2) Keep dividing until the quotient is 1.
3) The divisors are the factors in the prime factorization.

Use a *step diagram* to find the prime factorization of 75.

$$\begin{array}{r} 3|75 \\ 5|25 \\ 5|5 \\ 1 \end{array}$$

The prime factorization of 60 is $2 \cdot 2 \cdot 3 \cdot 5$, or $2^2 \cdot 3 \cdot 5$.

The prime factorization of 75 is $3 \cdot 5 \cdot 5$, or $3 \cdot 5^2$.

Use a step diagram to find the prime factorization.

**5.** 48
$2^4 \cdot 3$

**6.** 24
$2^3 \cdot 3$

**7.** 40
$2^3 \cdot 5$

**8.** 98
$2 \cdot 7^2$

---

## Challenge
### A Different Point of View

Create two more factor trees with different factors for each number. Possible answers are given.

**1.**

Prime factorization of 225: $3^2 \cdot 5^2$

**2.**

Prime factorization of 504: $2^3 \cdot 3^2 \cdot 7$

**3.** In 1742, Christian Goldbach wrote his now famous Goldbach's Conjecture, which states that every even number greater than 2 can be represented as the sum of 2 primes. Although this conjecture is still an open question, it can be supported. Choose 3 even numbers greater than 2 to help support Goldbach's Conjecture.

Possible answer: $12 = 7 + 5; 32 = 19 + 13; 44 = 13 + 31$

**4.** Goldbach also made a conjecture that every odd number is the sum of 3 primes. Choose 3 odd numbers to support this conjecture.

Possible answer: $13 = 3 + 5 + 5; 15 = 5 + 5 + 5; 33 = 23 + 5 + 5$

---

## Problem Solving
### Prime Factorization

Write the correct answer.

**1.** The width of a swimming pool (in feet) is a prime number greater than 10. The width and length of the pool are factors of 408. What are the dimensions of the pool?

<u>17 ft by 24 ft</u>

**2.** The area of the dining room at Thomas Jefferson's home in Monticello is about 342 square feet. If the approximate length of one side is a prime number less than 25, what are the approximate dimensions of the room?

<u>19 ft by 18 ft</u>

**3.** A university has a lounge that can be converted into a meeting hall for 250 people. If the hall is filled and everyone is in equal groups, what are the different ways the people can be grouped so that there are no more than 10 groups?

<u>5 groups of 50; 2 groups of 125;</u>
<u>10 groups of 25</u>

**4.** You want to read a mystery that has 435 pages. If you read the same number of pages per day and the number is a prime number greater than 20, how many pages per day will you read?

<u>29 pages per day for</u>
<u>15 days</u>

Choose the letter of the best answer.

**5.** There are 228 seventh graders. Each seventh-grade homeroom starts the year with the same number of students and has at least 15 students. What is the least number of rooms that are needed?

A 17
B 19
Ⓒ 12
D 21

**6.** Solve this riddle: I am a number whose prime factors are all the prime numbers between 6 and 15. No factor is repeated. What number am I?

F 9,009
G 91
Ⓗ 1,001
J 6,006

**7.** What is the prime factorization of 1,485?

Ⓐ 3 • 3 • 3 • 5 • 11
B 3 • 3 • 5 • 5 • 11
C 3 • 5 • 9 • 11
D 5 • 11 • 27

**8.** Solve this riddle: I am a prime factor of 39 and 65. What number am I?

F 3
G 5
H 11
Ⓙ 13

42  Holt Middle School Math  Course 2

---

## Puzzles, Twisters & Teasers
### Can You Find All the Words?

Solve the word search, then find the word from the list that best completes the riddle.

step  unique  composite  factor  factorization
exponent  tree  prime  diagram  Hajratwala

```
P R I M E F U N I Q U E P
C W E S A H D C B N U O F
T Y P L M A S X D S R W K
E R T Y U J C F T S Y C B
F A C T O R I Z A T I O N
A S Z R A A Q W R E I M F
C G B E X T D S A P B P M
T N M E A W N J I L K O C
O W E R T A T H N B V S I
R Y U I O L C V B N M I L
A S E D I A G R A M F T W
W S C E X P O N E N T E J
```

What was the mathematician's favorite food?

<u>P</u> <u>R</u> <u>I</u> <u>M</u> <u>E</u> rib

43  Holt Middle School Math  Course 2

---

## Exploration Recording Sheet
### Greatest Common Factor

At RFK Middle School there are 48 members of the grade 6 band, 60 members of the grade 7 band, and 36 members of the grade 8 band. Each band marches in a rectangular array of columns.

**1.** One possible formation for the 48 members of the grade 6 band is shown. Draw all possible formations of the grade 6 band.

1 × 48, 2 × 24, 3 × 16, 4 × 12, 6 × 8, 8 × 6, 12 × 4, 16 × 3, 24 × 2 and 48 × 1

**2.** One possible formation for the 60 members of the grade 7 band is shown. Draw all possible formations of the grade 7 band.

1 × 60, 2 × 30, 3 × 20, 4 × 15, 5 × 12, 6 × 10, 10 × 6, 12 × 5, 15 × 4, 20 × 3, 30 × 2 and 60 × 1

**3.** One possible formation for the 36 members of the grade 8 band is shown. Draw all possible formations of the grade 8 band.

1 × 36, 2 × 18, 3 × 12, 4 × 9, 6 × 6, 9 × 4, 12 × 3, 18 × 2 and 36 × 1

**4.** How can the band director put all three bands together in separate rectangular blocks that have the same number of columns and the greatest number of columns possible? Sketch a diagram of this formation.

<u>The formation will have 12 columns for each</u>
<u>grade. 6th = 12 × 4, 7th = 12 × 5 and</u>
<u>8th = 12 × 3</u>

**Think and Discuss**

**5. Compare** your solutions with the solutions of others. Check students' work.

**6. Discuss** how you decided what the final formation of all three grades should look like.

<u>Possible answer: The final formation should include as many columns as</u>
<u>possible, so choose as many of the common prime factors as possible:</u>
<u>2, 2 and 3.</u>

45  Holt Middle School Math  Course 2

---

## Practice A
### Greatest Common Factor

Draw a line to the greatest common factor (GCF). For Exercises 1–10, choose from A–K; for Exercises 11–20, choose from M–W.

| | | | |
|---|---|---|---|
| 1. 21, 35 | A. 3 | 11. 18, 48 | M. 16 |
| 2. 12, 32 | B. 7 | 12. 10, 25 | N. 60 |
| 3. 27, 66 | C. 5 | 13. 120, 180 | P. 6 |
| 4. 6, 12, 30 | D. 4 | 14. 16, 48, 80 | Q. 12 |
| 5. 20, 45, 75 | E. 9 | 15. 6, 16, 30 | R. 5 |
| 6. 27, 36, 45 | F. 6 | 16. 60, 84, 120 | S. 3 |
| 7. 25, 75, 100 | G. 19 | 17. 42, 63, 84 | T. 9 |
| 8. 38, 57 | H. 8 | 18. 64, 96 | U. 2 |
| 9. 32, 40, 120 | J. 25 | 19. 18, 99, 135 | V. 7 |
| 10. 36, 48, 60 | K. 12 | 20. 24, 45, 90 | W. 32 |

**21.** A jewelry designer is making identical bracelets. She has 21 blue beads and 14 red beads. What is the greatest number of bracelets she can make using all of the beads?

<u>7 bracelets</u>

**22.** A florist is preparing identical flower baskets for a banquet. He has 72 tulips and 60 roses. What is the greatest number of flower baskets he can prepare using all of the tulips and roses?

<u>12 flower baskets</u>

46  Holt Middle School Math  Course 2

---

**138**  Holt Middle School Math  Course 2

**Find the greatest common factor (GCF).**

**1.** 12, 15     **2.** 22, 33     **3.** 63, 45

3        11        9

**4.** 15, 50     **5.** 18, 81     **6.** 18, 48

5        9        6

**7.** 20, 24     **8.** 14, 42, 49     **9.** 3, 6, 9

4        7        3

**10.** 16, 24, 30     **11.** 16, 40, 88     **12.** 42, 70

2        8        14

**13.** 25, 125, 200     **14.** 26, 39, 52     **15.** 36, 100

25        13        4

**16.** 35, 77     **17.** 56, 84     **18.** 14, 49, 56, 84

7        28        7

**19.** 30, 75, 60, 90     **20.** 12, 38, 40, 94     **21.** 48, 66, 96, 102

15        2        6

**22.** Volunteers are preparing identical backpacks for refugees. There are 32 maps and 24 dictionaries to use for the backpacks. What is the greatest number of backpacks they can prepare using all of the maps and dictionaries?

8 backpacks

**23.** Alyssa is preparing identical fruit baskets. There are 36 oranges and 60 apples to use for the baskets. What is the greatest number of fruit baskets she can prepare using all of the oranges and apples?

12 baskets

 Holt Middle School Math Course 2

**Find the greatest common factor (GCF).**

**1.** 45, 75     **2.** 24, 56, 72     **3.** 14, 18, 22

15        8        2

**4.** 60, 80, 120     **5.** 32, 64, 80     **6.** 32, 40, 120

20        16        8

**7.** 55, 115     **8.** 64, 96     **9.** 14, 35, 56, 77

5        32        7

**10.** Which pair of numbers has a GCF that is a prime number, 91 and 117 or 84 and 156?

91 and 117 have a GCF of 13.

**11.** Which pair of numbers has a GCF that is a prime number, 54 and 99 or 80 and 114?

80 and 114 have a GCF of 2.

**12.** Which pair of numbers has a GCF that is a prime number, 70 and 112 or 68 and 187?

68 and 187 have a GCF of 17.

**13.** Carvin is preparing identical breakfast gift sets. There are 18 boxes of pancake mix and 27 jars of jam. What is the greatest number of gift sets he can prepare using all of the pancake mix and jam?

9 gift sets

**14.** Amelia is decorating identical frames. She has 75 red feathers and 30 blue tiles. What is the greatest number of frames she can decorate using all of the feathers and tiles?

15 frames

**15.** A jeweler is making identical necklaces. He has 24 gold beads and 144 colored glass beads. What is the greatest number of necklaces he can make using all the gold beads and glass beads?

24 necklaces

 Holt Middle School Math Course 2

The **greatest common factor** (GCF) of a group of numbers is the greatest number that can divide each of the numbers without having a remainder.

Use a list to find the GCF of 45, 60, and 75.
List all the factors of each number.

45: 1, 3, 5, 9, 15, 45
60: 1, 2, 3, 4, 5, 6, 10, 12, 15, 20, 30, 60
75: 1, 3, 5, 15, 25, 75

The common factors are 1, 3, 5, and 15.
The GCF is 15.

**List the factors of each number. Find the greatest common factor (GCF).**

**1.** 9: 1, 3, 9
24: 1, 2, 3, 4, 6, 8, 12, 24
GCF = 3

**2.** 18: 1, 2, 3, 6, 9, 18
54: 1, 2, 3, 6, 9, 18, 27, 54
GCF = 18

**3.** 45: 1, 3, 5, 9, 15, 45
55: 1, 5, 11, 55
GCF = 5

**4.** 12: 1, 2, 3, 4, 6, 12
20: 1, 2, 4, 5, 10, 20
GCF = 4

**5.** 6: 1, 2, 3, 6
12: 1, 2, 3, 4, 6, 12
24: 1, 2, 3, 4, 6, 8, 12, 24
GCF = 6

**6.** 6: 1, 2, 3, 6
18: 1, 2, 3, 6, 9, 18
27: 1, 3, 9, 27
GCF = 3

**Find the greatest common factor (GCF).**

**7.** 27, 45     **8.** 14, 18     **9.** 12, 30     **10.** 10, 45, 70

9        2        6        5

 Holt Middle School Math Course 2

There are 24 students in the seventh grade and 36 students in the eighth grade. Solve each problem below about their school trip. Then use your solutions to complete the permission slip each student must have signed in order to go on the trip.

**1.** The students will visit the zoo, the museum, or the planetarium. Each class will buy its own tickets. Both classes must agree upon the trip that will cost the least. Use the table at right to decide which trip the students will choose.

| Trip | Single Tickets | Group Rate | Number of Tickets per Group |
|---|---|---|---|
| Zoo | $8 | $24 | 6 |
| Museum | $5 | $12 | 4 |
| Planetarium | $4 | $30 | 12 |

**2.** The principal will provide transportation for both classes. The school PTA will pay the cost but wants the most cost-efficient method of transportation. Use the table at right to decide which method of transportation the PTA will choose.

| Type of Transportation | Number of Passengers | Cost |
|---|---|---|
| Mini-bus | 12 | $35 |
| School Bus | 70 | $185 |
| Mini-van | 10 | $30 |

**3.** The class student council will provide lunch for each class. Each class must agree on the lowest price and then buy at least one lunch pack per student. Use the table at right to decide which lunch deal the students will choose.

| Lunch | Number of Lunches per Pack | Cost per Pack |
|---|---|---|
| Sandwich and Juice Packs | 6 | $15 |
| Yogurt and Drink Packs | 8 | $20 |
| Soup and Sandwich Packs | 4 | $12 |

To the Seventh and Eighth-grade Parents:
On Friday, your child will be taking a school trip to the planetarium. The school will pay $60 for the seventh-graders' tickets and $90 for the eighth-graders' tickets. The PTA has graciously offered to pay $175 for 5 [number] mini-buses [vehicles] to transport the students. Each class's student council will pay for its class's lunches. Both classes will buy 10 [number] sandwich and juice [type] packs at a total cost of $60 for the seventh graders and $90 for the eighth graders.

_____ Parent's signature for student's permission

 Holt Middle School Math Course 2

## Problem Solving
### Greatest Common Factor

**Write the correct answer.**

**1.** Fabric is sold in stores from bolts that are 45 or 60 inches wide. What is the width of the widest strips of fabric you can cut from either bolt without wasting any of the fabric if each strip has the same width?

15 inches

**2.** The parents are making sandwiches for the class picnic. They have 72 turkey slices, 48 cheese slices, and 96 tomato slices. What is the greatest number of sandwiches they can make if each sandwich has the same filling?

24 sandwiches

**3.** Two bicycle enthusiasts are leaving Cincinnati at the same time. One is biking 840 miles to Boston. The other is biking 440 miles to Atlanta. What is the greatest number of miles a day each can bike if they want to cover equal distances each day?

40 miles per day

**4.** A fruit salad made on a TV cooking program requires chunks of cantaloupe and honeydew. What is the greatest number of servings you can make using all of the fruit if you have 30 chunks of cantaloupe and 42 chunks of honeydew?

6 servings

**Choose the letter for the best answer.**

**5.** Ari is making patriotic pins. He has 105 red ribbons, 147 white ribbons, and 189 blue ribbons. What is the greatest number of identical pins he can make if he uses all his ribbons?
A 52 pins    C 93 pins
B 19 pins    (D) 21 pins

**6.** Cheryce is making fruit baskets. She has 60 bananas, 72 pears, 96 apples, and 108 oranges. What is the greatest number of equal baskets she can make with the fruit?
F 3 baskets    (H) 12 baskets
G 6 baskets    J 24 baskets

**7.** There are 100 senators and 435 representatives in the United States Congress. How many identical groups could be formed from all the senators and representatives?
A 1 group
(B) 5 groups
C 10 groups
D 15 groups

**8.** There are 14 baseball teams in the American League and 16 teams in the National League. There are 30 National Hockey League teams. If equal groups of teams are formed, how many hockey teams will be in each group?
F 3 hockey teams
G 8 hockey teams
H 7 hockey teams
(J) 15 hockey teams

51    Holt Middle School Math  Course 2

---

## Puzzles, Twisters & Teasers
### That's the Greatest!

**Find the greatest common factor for each set of numbers. Then use the decoder to answer the riddle below.**

**1.** 24, 36, 48, 54   12   L
**2.** 30, 45, 60, 75   15   E
**3.** 20, 40, 50, 120   10   K
**4.** 4, 6, 10, 22   2   N
**5.** 6, 15, 33, 48   3   A
**6.** 14, 21, 35, 70   7   R
**7.** 2, 3, 4, 5, 7   1   O
**8.** 18, 45, 63, 81   9   C

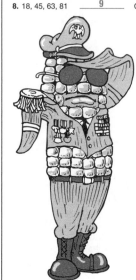

What do you call a piece of corn in the army?

A   C   O  R  N
3   9   1   7   2

K   E   R  N  E  L
10  15  7  2  15  12

52    Holt Middle School Math  Course 2

---

## Exploration Recording Sheet
### Least Common Multiple

Earl, Mindy, and Sarah run laps around a park.

- **Mindy** can complete one lap in **24 minutes**.  ⟶ 24
- **Earl** can complete one lap in **36 minutes**.  ⟶ 36
- **Sarah** can complete one lap in **18 minutes**.  ⟶ 18

**1.** After how many minutes will **Mindy** and **Earl** end a lap together?  72  ⟶ 24 ⟶ 36

**2.** After how many minutes will **Earl** and **Sarah** end a lap together?  36  ⟶ 36 ⟶ 18

**3.** After how many minutes will **Mindy** and **Sarah** end a lap together?  72  ⟶ 24 ⟶ 18

**4.** What are three different times at which they can all end a lap together?

Possible answer: 72, 144, 216

**Think and Discuss**

**5. Compare** your solutions with the solutions of others.

Check students' work.

**6. Discuss** how you found your answers to number 4.

Possible answer: Because 72 is the least common multiple, multiples of 72 are the times they would all end a lap together.

54    Holt Middle School Math  Course 2

---

## Practice A
### Least Common Multiple

**Find the correct least common multiple (LCM) for each set of numbers below. Match each LCM with a number in the box.**

| 21 | 60 | 33 | 20 | 35 | 75 |
|----|----|----|----|----|----|
| 42 | 20 | 40 | 78 | 99 | 36 |

**1.** 3, 7   21
**2.** 4, 5   20
**3.** 10, 12   60

**4.** 15, 25   75
**5.** 3, 11   33
**6.** 9, 12, 18   36

**7.** 6, 7, 21   42
**8.** 5, 8, 20   40
**9.** 2, 26, 39   78

**Find the LCM.**

**10.** 10, 18, 45   90
**11.** 5, 6, 20   60
**12.** 10, 15, 30   30

**13.** 2, 4, 7, 8   56
**14.** 3, 9, 12   36
**15.** 2, 5, 7, 10   70

**16.** 5, 9, 18   90
**17.** 4, 10, 12, 15   60
**18.** 4, 9, 12, 18   36

**19.** 8, 16, 32   32
**20.** 5, 15, 20   60
**21.** 2, 6, 18, 21   126

**22.** Carrie and Lance are playing the drums for the band. In the song, Carrie beats the bass drum every 3 beats. Lance beats the snare drum every 5 beats. On what beat will they first play their drums together?

15th beat

**23.** Domingo is helping his father paint some boards. Domingo paints a board every 12 minutes. His father paints a board every 8 minutes. If they start together, how long before they will finish painting a board at the same time?

24 minutes

55    Holt Middle School Math  Course 2

---

**Practice B**
*Least Common Multiple*

**Find the least common multiple (LCM).**

| | | |
|---|---|---|
| **1.** 8, 10 <br> 40 | **2.** 10, 15 <br> 30 | **3.** 6, 9 <br> 18 |
| **4.** 12, 16 <br> 48 | **5.** 18, 30 <br> 90 | **6.** 5, 11 <br> 55 |
| **7.** 15, 45 <br> 45 | **8.** 7, 28 <br> 28 | **9.** 4, 14 <br> 28 |
| **10.** 3, 10, 12 <br> 60 | **11.** 9, 36, 60 <br> 180 | **12.** 5, 15 <br> 15 |
| **13.** 7, 14, 49 <br> 98 | **14.** 8, 12, 24, 96 <br> 96 | **15.** 5, 25, 30 <br> 150 |
| **16.** 5, 9, 18 <br> 90 | **17.** 4, 10, 12, 15 <br> 60 | **18.** 4, 9, 12, 18 <br> 36 |
| **19.** 4, 12, 24, 36 <br> 72 | **20.** 24, 30, 48, 60 <br> 240 | **21.** 5, 9, 15, 18 <br> 90 |

**22.** Jasmine is helping her father plant trees to create a border around the back yard. Jasmine plants a tree every 25 minutes, and her father plants a tree every 15 minutes. If they started together, how long before they would finish planting a tree at the same time?

75 minutes

**23.** Two dancers are rehearsing in a studio. One dancer's routine lasts 12 minutes. The other dancer's routine lasts 15 minutes. If they start together and take no breaks between their routines, how long before they start together again?

60 minutes

**24.** Evan and Renzo are swimming laps in the pool. It takes Evan 8 minutes to complete 1 lap and Renzo 6 minutes to complete 1 lap. They start together at the tops of their lanes. In how many minutes will they be together again at the tops of their lanes?

24 minutes

56 Holt Middle School Math Course 2

---

**Practice C**
*Least Common Multiple*

**Find the least common multiple (LCM).**

| | | |
|---|---|---|
| **1.** 9, 12 <br> 36 | **2.** 18, 60 <br> 180 | **3.** 9, 15 <br> 45 |
| **4.** 20, 100 <br> 100 | **5.** 7, 11 <br> 77 | **6.** 8, 12, 16 <br> 48 |
| **7.** 3, 7, 21 <br> 21 | **8.** 40, 100 <br> 200 | **9.** 5, 9, 18 <br> 90 |
| **10.** 2, 26, 39 <br> 78 | **11.** 5, 8, 12 <br> 120 | **12.** 20, 40, 50 <br> 200 |
| **13.** 8, 9, 12 <br> 72 | **14.** 4, 6, 9, 12 <br> 36 | **15.** 3, 9, 12, 72 <br> 72 |
| **16.** 4, 10, 12 <br> 60 | **17.** 5, 20, 25, 50 <br> 100 | **18.** 4, 7, 8, 28 <br> 56 |
| **19.** 15, 20, 30 <br> 60 | **20.** 2, 6, 9, 21 <br> 126 | **21.** 10, 32, 64, 80 <br> 320 |

**22.** Josh and Eva are packing first-aid supplies. It takes Josh 12 minutes to fill a box with bandages. It takes Eva 8 minutes to fill a box with antibiotics. If they start packing boxes at the same time, how long will it be before they start filling a new box at the same time?

24 minutes

**23.** Sadie is helping her mother stain some shelves. Sadie stains a shelf every 25 minutes. Her mother stains a shelf every 15 minutes. If they start together, how long will it be before they finish staining a shelf at the same time?

75 minutes

**24.** It takes Amanda 14 minutes to climb up the hill and sled down. It takes Alvin 12 minutes to climb up the hill and sled down. If they start up the hill at the same time, how long will it be before they meet again at the starting point?

84 minutes

57 Holt Middle School Math Course 2

---

**Reteach**
*Least Common Multiple*

The **least common multiple** (LCM) of two numbers is the least multiple that the two numbers have in common.

- To list the multiples of a number, multiply the number by 1, 2, 3, and so on.

| | 8 • 1 | 8 • 2 | 8 • 3 | 8 • 4 | 8 • 5 |
|---|---|---|---|---|---|
| Multiples of 8 | 8 | 16 | 24 | 32 | 40 |

| | 6 • 1 | 6 • 2 | 6 • 3 | 6 • 4 | 6 • 5 |
|---|---|---|---|---|---|
| Multiples of 6 | 6 | 12 | 18 | 24 | 30 |

- To find the least common multiple of 6 and 8, list several multiples of each number.

**Step 1:** List multiples of the greater number. → Multiples of 8: 8 16 **24** 32 40

**Step 2:** List the multiples of the lesser number until you find a multiple that is common to each list. → Multiples of 6: 6 12 18 **24**

Since 24 is the first number common to both lists, it is the least common multiple. So the LCM of 6 and 8 is 24.

**Find the least common multiple (LCM).**

**1.** 4, 9
Multiples of 9: 9, 18, 27, 36, 45, 54
Multiples of 4: 4, 8, 12, 16, 20, 24, 28, 32, 36
LCM of 4 and 9: 36

**2.** 6, 7
Multiples of 7: 7, 14, 21, 28, 35, 42, 49, 56
Multiples of 6: 6, 12, 18, 24, 30, 36, 42
LCM of 6 and 7: 42

**3.** 15, 20
Multiples of 20: 20, 40, 60, 80, 100
Multiples of 15: 15, 30, 45, 60
LCM of 15 and 20: 60

| | | |
|---|---|---|
| **4.** 12, 18 36 | **5.** 16, 20 80 | **6.** 4, 6, 9 36 |

58 Holt Middle School Math Course 2

---

**Challenge**
*Multiple Solutions*

Write the two numbers from each box that have the lowest least common multiple. Then write the LCM.

| | | | |
|---|---|---|---|
| **1.** 5 12 / 6 8 | Numbers: 6; 12 <br> LCM: 12 | **2.** 2 7 / 9 10 | Numbers: 2; 10 <br> LCM: 10 |
| **3.** 2 10 / 5 3 | Numbers: 2; 3 <br> LCM: 6 | **4.** 7 2 / 10 12 | Numbers: 2; 10 <br> LCM: 10 |
| **5.** 6 4 / 7 5 | Numbers: 4; 6 <br> LCM: 12 | **6.** 9 10 / 15 45 | Numbers: 10; 15 <br> LCM: 30 |
| **7.** 8 10 / 6 5 | Numbers: 5; 10 <br> LCM: 10 | **8.** 24 35 / 32 14 | Numbers: 14; 35 <br> LCM: 70 |
| **9.** 15 10 / 7 8 | Numbers: 10; 15 <br> LCM: 30 | **10.** 3 10 / 12 7 | Numbers: 3; 12 <br> LCM: 12 |

Use the table at the bottom of the page to solve the riddle. In the middle row, write the LCM of each exercise above the exercise number. Then choose the letter from the Answer Key that matches the LCM and write it in the appropriate box.

**Answer Key**

| C | A | T | E | H |
|---|---|---|---|---|
| 70 | 6 | 30 | 12 | 10 |

**11.** What animal copies from the others on a math test?

| T | H | E | | C | H | E | E | T | A | H |
|---|---|---|---|---|---|---|---|---|---|---|
| 30 | 10 | 12 | | 70 | 10 | 12 | 12 | 30 | 6 | 10 |
| 9 | 4 | 5 | | 8 | 2 | 1 | 5 | 6 | 3 | 7 |

59 Holt Middle School Math Course 2

---

## Problem Solving
### Least Common Multiple

**Write the correct answer.**

**1.** Earth revolves around the sun every year. Jupiter revolves around the sun every 12 years. If Earth and Jupiter passed the same point of the sun sometime in 2002, when will they pass that point together again?

2014

**2.** House representatives are elected every 2 years. The President of the United States is elected every 4 years. Both will be elected in 2004. When is the next year after 2004 both will be elected?

2008

**3.** A cat runs a mile every 2 minutes. A squirrel runs a mile every 5 minutes. A cat and a squirrel start together running around a 1-mile track. How long will it be before they meet at the starting point?

10 minutes

**4.** A car manual recommends changing the oil every 5,000 miles and inspecting the engine coolant system every 15,000 miles. At how many miles will both be done together for the first time? for the second time?

15,000 mi; 30,000 mi

**Choose the letter for the best answer.**

**5.** Mr. Walters receives a dividend every 5 months and a royalty payment every 6 months. He received both in January 2002. When is the next time he would receive both payments in the same month?

A January 2003
B April 2004
C July 2002
**D** July 2004

**6.** Rag Rite Cloth Store always rounds amounts less than whole yards up to the next yard for ribbon purchases. The ribbon that you want to buy comes in rolls of 8 feet. How many rolls should you buy to get the best buy?

F 1 roll
G 2 rolls
**H** 3 rolls
J 4 rolls

**7.** The sanitation department picks up recyclable plastics every 3 days. The paper recycling center picks up papers every 4 days. They both picked up on May 4. When will they next pick up on the same day?

A May 7
B May 12
C May 11
**D** May 16

**8.** Hal and Jess both volunteer at the local nursing home. Hal volunteers every 6 days, and Jess volunteers every 8 days. They were both there on Monday. In how many days will they both volunteer together again?

F in 14 days
**G** in 24 days
H in 48 days
J in 2 days

60 Holt Middle School Math **Course 2**

---

## Puzzles, Twisters & Teasers
### A Common Cause!

Find the least common multiple for each set of numbers. Spell out the answers to solve the crossword puzzle.

**Across**
1. 3, 5
4. 9, 12
6. 10, 4
7. 2, 5
9. 6, 14

**Down**
1. 3, 9, 15
2. 4, 6, 12
3. 6, 9
5. 4, 7
6. 3, 7
8. 15, 20

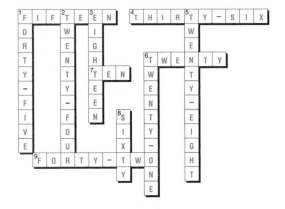

61 Holt Middle School Math **Course 2**

---

## Exploration Recording Sheet
### Variables and Algebraic Expressions

Suzanne entered a walk-a-thon for a local charity. Her sponsor provided the $20 entry fee and will provide $4 for each mile she walks.

**1.** Complete the table.

| Miles Walked | Expression | Amount (s) |
|---|---|---|
| 1 | 20 + 4(1) | 24 |
| 2 | 20 + 4(2) | 28 |
| 3 | 20 + 4(3) | 32 |
| 4 | 20 + 4(4) | 36 |
| 5 | 20 + 4(5) | 40 |
| 6 | 20 + 4(6) | 44 |

**2.** If Suzanne walks 12 miles, how much money will she collect for the charity?

$68

**3.** Suppose Suzanne wants to give $100 to the charity. How many miles must she walk?

20 miles

**Think and Discuss**

**4.** **Explain** how the number of miles walked is used to determine the amount of money collected.

Possible answer: The number of miles walked is multiplied by 4, and that product is added to 20.

**5.** **Describe** how to write an expression for the amount of money collected if the number of miles walked is replaced by the variable $m$.

Replace the number of miles walked with the variable $m$: $20 + 4m$

64 Holt Middle School Math **Course 2**

---

## Practice A
### Variables and Algebraic Expressions

Find the value of $n + 3$ for each value of $n$.

**1.** $n = 4$   **2.** $n = 7$   **3.** $n = 0$   **4.** $n = 32$
7   10   3   35

Find the value of $x - 9$ for each value of $x$.

**5.** $x = 12$   **6.** $x = 57$   **7.** $x = 19$   **8.** $x = 100$
3   48   10   91

Find the value of each expression using the given value for each variable.

**9.** $3n$ for $n = 4$   **10.** $x + 8$ for $x = 8$   **11.** $9p - 6$ for $p = 2$
12   16   12

**12.** $n \div 5$ for $n = 35$   **13.** $6x + 18$ for $x = 0$   **14.** $s - 7$ for $s = 8$
7   18   1

**15.** $3w + 5$ for $w = 3$   **16.** $c - 9$ for $c = 12$   **17.** $2a \div 3$ for $a = 6$
14   3   4

**18.** $y + z$ for $y = 10$ and $z = 20$   **19.** $3w - 2v$ for $w = 7$ and $v = 8$
30   5

**20.** $4a \div b$ for $a = 6$ and $b = 4$   **21.** $5s + 4t$ for $s = 3$ and $t = 4$
6   31

**22.** The expression $7w$ gives the number of days in $w$ weeks. Find the value of $7w$ for $w = 20$. How many days are there in 20 weeks?
140 days

**23.** A cat can run as fast as $m \div 2$ miles per minute in $m$ minutes. Find the value of $m \div 2$ for $m = 10$. How many miles can a cat run in 10 minutes?
5 miles

**24.** Tyrone works 8 hours a day. You can use the expression $8d$ to find the total number of hours he works in $d$ days. How many hours does he work in 5 days?
40 hours

65 Holt Middle School Math **Course 2**

---

142 Holt Middle School Math   Course 2

Evaluate $n - 5$ for each value of $n$.

**1.** $n = 8$     **2.** $n = 121$     **3.** $n = 32$     **4.** $n = 59$
   3        116        27        54

Evaluate each algebraic expression for the given variable values.

**5.** $3n + 15$ for $n = 4$    **6.** $h \div 12$ for $h = 60$    **7.** $32x - 32$ for $x = 2$
   27        5        32

**8.** $\frac{c}{2}$ for $c = 24$    **9.** $(n \div 2)5$ for $n = 14$    **10.** $8p + 148$ for $p = 15$
   12        35        268

**11.** $e^2 - 7$ for $e = 8$    **12.** $3d^2 + d$ for $d = 5$    **13.** $40 - 4k^3$ for $k = 2$
   57        80        8

**14.** $2y - z$ for $y = 21$ and $z = 19$    **15.** $3h^2 + 8m$ for $h = 3$ and $m = 2$
   23        43

**16.** $18 \div a + b \div 9$ for $a = 6$ and $b = 45$    **17.** $10x - 4y$ for $x = 14$ and $y = 5$
   8        120

**18.** You can find the area of a rectangle with the expression $lw$ where $l$ represents the length and $w$ represents the width. What is the area of the rectangle at right in square feet?

5 ft

2 ft

   10 square feet

**19.** Rita drove an average of 55 mi/h on her trip to the mountains. You can use the expression $55h$ to find out how many miles she drove in $h$ hours. If she drove for 5 hours, how many miles did she drive?

   275 miles

   **66**      Holt Middle School Math   Course 2

---

Evaluate each algebraic expression for the given variable values.

**1.** $3n + 4n$ for $n = 8$      **2.** $\frac{6s}{5}$ for $s = 25$
   56          30

**3.** $q^2 + 5q - 11$ for $q = 4$      **4.** $\frac{350}{d} + 4d + 7$ for $d = 10$
   25          82

**5.** $9x + 2x^2 + 2$ for $x = 2$      **6.** $8m^2 + 7 - 2m$ for $m = 3$
   28          73

**7.** $4(h + k)$ for $h = 3$ and $k = 55$      **8.** $\frac{6r}{4} + 5s$ for $r = 8$ and $s = 18$
   232          102

**9.** $6a - 2b^2$ for $a = 9$ and $b = 5$      **10.** $6h - 20g$ for $h = 1{,}500$ and $g = 200$
   4          5,000

**11.** $\frac{36}{m^2} + \frac{n^2}{4}$ for $m = 6$ and $n = 16$      **12.** $x^2 - 2x - y^2$ for $x = 15$ and $y = 2$
   65          191

**13.** $4d^3 + 6e^2 - \frac{8d}{2}$ for $d = 2$ and $e = 3$      **14.** $\frac{5r^2}{4} + \frac{4s}{3r}$ for $r = 4$ and $s = 9$
   78          23

**15.** You can find the volume of a rectangular prism with the expression $a \cdot b \cdot c$, where $a$ is the length, $b$ is the width, and $c$ is the height of the prism. What is the volume of the prism at right in cubic inches?

8 in.

3 in.   2 in.

   48 cubic inches

**16.** You can use the expression $5m$ to find out how many seconds it takes a sound to travel $m$ miles through the air. However, through water, sound takes $m$ seconds to travel $m$ miles. Use the expression $5m - m$ to find out how much longer will it take a sound to travel 8 miles in air than in water.

   32 seconds longer

   **67**      Holt Middle School Math   Course 2

---

A **variable** is a letter that represents a number than can change in an expression. When you **evaluate** an algebraic expression, you substitute the value given for the variable in the expression.

• Algebraic expression: $x - 3$

The value of the expression depends on the value of the variable $x$.

If $x = 7 \rightarrow 7 - 3 = 4$
If $x = 11 \rightarrow 11 - 3 = 8$
If $x = 15 \rightarrow 15 - 3 = 12$

• Evaluate $4n + 1$ for $n = 5$.
Replace the variable $n$ with 5. $\rightarrow 4(5) + 1 = 20 + 1 = 21$

Evaluate each expression for the given value.

**1.** $a + 7$ for $a = 3$      **2.** $k - 5$ for $k = 13$
   $a + 7 = 3 + 7 = $ __10__      $k - 5 = $ __13__ $- 5 = $ __8__

**3.** $y \div 3$ for $y = 6$      **4.** $12 + m$ for $m = 9$
   $y \div 3 = $ __6__ $\div 3 = $ __2__      $12 + m = $ __12__ $+$ __9__ $=$ __21__

**5.** $3n - 2$ for $n = 5$
   $3n - 2 = 3($ __5__ $) - 2 = $ __15__ $- 2 = $ __13__

**6.** $5x + 4$ for $x = 4$
   $5x + 4 = 5($ __4__ $) +$ __4__ $=$ __20__ $+$ __4__ $=$ __24__

**7.** $c - 9$ for $c = 11$    **8.** $b + 16$ for $b = 4$    **9.** $a - 4$ for $a = 9$
   2        20        5

**10.** $25 - g$ for $g = 12$    **11.** $w + 5$ for $w = 2$    **12.** $3 + s$ for $s = 8$
   13        7        11

**13.** $7q$ for $q = 10$    **14.** $2y + 9$ for $y = 8$    **15.** $6x - 3$ for $x = 1$
   70        25        3

   **68**      Holt Middle School Math   Course 2

---

Complete each table with four expressions that have the same value. Use each given value of $n$.

**1.**

| Expression Value 32 | Value of $n$ 4 |
|---|---|
| Addition expression: $n + 28$ | |
| Subtraction expression: $36 - n$ | |
| Multiplication expression: $8n$ | |
| Division expression: $128 \div n$ | |

**2.**

| Expression Value 96 | Value of $n$ 12 |
|---|---|
| Addition expression: $n + 84$ | |
| Subtraction expression: $108 - n$ | |
| Multiplication expression: $8n$ | |
| Division expression: $1{,}152 \div n$ | |

**3.**

| Expression Value 156 | Value of $n$ 6 |
|---|---|
| Addition expression: $n + 150$ | |
| Subtraction expression: $162 - n$ | |
| Multiplication expression: $26n$ | |
| Division expression: $936 \div n$ | |

**4.**

| Expression Value 98 | Value of $n$ 14 |
|---|---|
| Addition expression: $n + 84$ | |
| Subtraction expression: $112 - n$ | |
| Multiplication expression: $7n$ | |
| Division expression: $1{,}372 \div n$ | |

**5.**

| Expression Value 57 | Value of $n$ 12 |
|---|---|
| Addition expression: $n + 45$ | |
| Subtraction expression: $69 - n$ | |
| Multiplication expression: $4.75n$ | |
| Division expression: $684 \div n$ | |

**6.**

| Expression Value 248 | Value of $n$ 124 |
|---|---|
| Addition expression: $n + 124$ | |
| Subtraction expression: $372 - n$ | |
| Multiplication expression: $2n$ | |
| Division expression: $30{,}752 \div n$ | |

   **69**      Holt Middle School Math   Course 2

   **143**      Holt Middle School Math   Course 2

## Problem Solving
### Variables and Expressions

**Write the correct answer.**

1. In 2000, people in the United States watched television an average of 29 hours per week. Use the expression 29w for w = 4 to find out about how many hours per month this is.

   about 116 hours

2. Find the value of the variable w in the expression 29w to find the average number of hours people watched television in a year. Find the value of the expression.

   52; 1,508 hours

3. The expression y + 45 gives the year when a person will be 45 years old, where y is the year of birth. When will a person born in 1992 be 45 years old?

   2037

4. The expression 24g gives the number of miles Guy's car can travel on g gallons of gas. If the car has 6 gallons of gas left, how much farther can he drive?

   144 miles

**Choose the letter for the best answer.**

5. Sam is 5 feet tall. The expression 0.5m + 60 can be used to calculate his height in inches if he grows an average of 0.5 inch each month. How tall will Sam be in 6 months?
   - A 56 inches
   - B 5 feet 6 inches
   - Ⓒ 63 inches
   - D 53 inches

6. The winner of the 1911 Indianapolis 500 auto race drove at a speed of about s − 56 mi/h, where s is the 2001 winning speed of about 131 mi/h. What was the approximate winning speed in 1911?
   - Ⓕ 75 mi/h
   - G 186 mi/h
   - H 85 mi/h
   - J 187 mi/h

7. The expression 1,587v gives the number of pounds of waste produced per person in the United States in v years. How many pounds of waste per person is produced in the United States in 6 years?
   - A 1,581 pounds
   - B 1,593 pounds
   - C 9,348 pounds
   - Ⓓ 9,522 pounds

8. The expression $1.25p + $3.50 can be used to calculate the total charge for faxing p pages at a business services store. How much would it cost to fax 8 pages?
   - F $12.50
   - G $4.75
   - Ⓗ $13.50
   - J $10.00

---

## Puzzles, Twisters & Teasers
### Movie Math!

Circle words from the list in the word search. Then find an extra word in the word search that best completes the riddle.

| expression | substitute | variable | value |
|---|---|---|---|
| constant | evaluate | algebra | algebraic |

```
V A L U E S D E X P R E S S I O N
Q A C V B N M V A S D F U B H U I
W L R L K J G A C T U P B V M A L
E G G I L S P L A S H W S I K L N
R E C V A R T U M J U I T C V G U
T B N H T B Q A S D F G I P O E U
Y R X O P N L T E R W T T Y T B E
U A V G T M K E U H B J U W Q R D
O I P O I U Y T F I J O T A X A G
P C O N S T A N T D F G E Z X C V
```

This Ron Howard movie was all wet.

S  P  L  A  S  H

---

## Exploration Recording Sheet
### Translate Words into Math

**Follow the steps below, showing your work for each step.**

**Step 1:** Choose any whole number between 1 and 10.

**Step 2:** Add to it the next two whole numbers that come after it.

**Step 3:** Divide the result by 3.

**Step 4:** Subtract the number that you began with.

**Step 5:** Tell what number you end with.

1. Compare your results with any other students who began with the same whole number for Step 1. Do your results agree?

   The result should be 1 for all who began with the same whole number.

2. Compare your results with any other students who did not begin with the same whole number for Step 1. Do your results agree?

   The result should be 1 for all who began with different whole numbers.

**Think and Discuss**

3. **Describe** the operation in step 2. What numbers are involved?

   Possible answer: The operation in Step 2 is the sum of 3 consecutive whole numbers, the first of which is between 1 and 10.

4. **Look for a pattern** in all the results. Describe what you find.

   All results should be 1.

---

## Practice A
### Translate Words Into Math

**Write as an algebraic expression.**

1. the sum of m and 8

   m + 8

2. the product of 3 and n

   3n

3. 4 less than x

   x − 4

4. the quotient of a number and 12

   a ÷ 12

5. 52 times a number

   52k

6. w less than 15

   15 − w

7. the sum of 13 and a number

   13 + e

8. the sum of 5 times p and 10

   5p + 10

9. the sum of 15 divided by b and 6

   15 ÷ b + 6

10. 12 less than the amount y divided by 2

    y ÷ 2 − 12

11. 26 increased by 12 times a number    26 + 12s

12. the difference of 2 times a number and 6    2a − 6

13. the product of h and 3, increased by 20    3h + 20

14. 18 less than the product of a number and 4    4n − 18

15. take away 32 from the product of 6 and a number    6z − 32

16. Used video games cost $25 each. Write an expression to find the cost of m video games.    25m

17. Sal earned $740 for n weeks of work. Write an expression for the amount he earned each week.    740 ÷ n

18. As of the 2000–2001 NBA season, Reggie Miller is the all-time leader in 3-point field goals made. He made n more field goals than Dale Ellis. Dale Ellis made 1,719 3-pointers. Write an expression to find the number of 3-pointers Reggie Miller made.    1,719 + n

19. The $2 bill has Thomas Jefferson on the front of it. Write an expression to find out how much money v bills with Thomas Jefferson on them would be worth.    2v

---

## Practice B
### 2-8 Translate Words Into Math

**Write as an algebraic expression.**

1. 125 decreased by a number
   $125 - n$

2. 359 more than $z$
   $z + 359$

3. the product of a number and 35
   $35f$

4. the quotient of 100 and $w$
   $100 \div w$

5. twice a number, plus 27
   $2r + 27$

6. 12 less than 15 times $x$
   $15x - 12$

7. the product of $e$ and 4, divided by 12
   $4e \div 12$

8. $y$ less than 18 times 6
   $18 \cdot 6 - y$

9. 48 more than the quotient of a number and 64   $m \div 64 + 48$

10. 500 less than the product of 4 and a number   $4t - 500$

11. the quotient of $p$ and 4, decreased by 320   $p \div 4 - 320$

12. 13 multiplied by the amount 60 minus $w$   $13(60 - w)$

13. the quotient of 45 and the sum of $c$ and 17   $45 \div (c + 17)$

14. twice the sum of a number and 600   $2(d + 600)$

15. There are twice as many flute players as there are trumpet players in the band. If there are $n$ flute players, write an expression to find out how many trumpet players there are.   $n \div 2$

16. The Nile River is the longest river in the world at 4,160 miles. A group of explorers traveled along the entire Nile in $x$ days. They traveled the same distance each day. Write an expression to find each day's distance.   $4{,}160 \div x$

17. A slice of pizza has 290 calories, and a stalk of celery has 5 calories. Write an expression to find out how many calories there are in $a$ slices of pizza and $b$ stalks of celery.   $290a + 5b$

18. Grant pays 10¢ per minute plus $5 per month for telephone long distance. Write an expression for $m$ minutes of long-distance calls in one month.   $0.10m + 5$

## Practice C
### 2-8 Translate Words Into Math

**Write as an algebraic expression.**

1. the product of 6 and the square of a number   $6n^2$

2. the square of the product of 6 and a number   $(6n)^2$

3. 4 times the sum of a number and 6,008   $4(r + 6{,}008)$

4. 200 less than half of a number   $y \div 2 - 200$

5. 3 times the difference of a number squared and 82   $3(n^2 - 82)$

6. 999 less than 45 increased by the product of a number and 85   $(45 + 85e) - 999$

**Write a verbal expression for each algebraic expression.** Possible answers given.

7. $2(4n)$   twice the product of a number and 4

8. $100 - \dfrac{54}{w}$   100 less the quotient of 54 and $w$

9. $r^2 + 4r + 7$   $r$ squared plus 4 times $r$, plus 7

10. $\dfrac{45}{5s^2}$   45 divided by the product of 5 and a number squared

11. An albatross can sleep while flying 25 mi/h. An albatross flew 3 miles awake and another $n$ hours asleep at 25 mi/h. Write an expression to find the distance flown.   $25n + 3$

12. You have $d$ dimes, $q$ quarters, and $n$ nickels. Write an expression to find the total amount of money.   $0.10d + 0.25q + 0.05n$

13. Four out of every 10 homes in the United States have a dog. Write an expression to find out how many dogs there are in $h$ homes.   $\dfrac{4h}{10}$

14. A waitress who worked $k$ hours earned $32 in tips. She gets an additional salary of $4.50 per hour. Write an expression to find the amount she earned.   $4.50k + 32$

## Reteach
### 2-8 Translate Words Into Math

Use the operation clues in a word phrase to translate word phrases into algebraic expressions.

| Addition | Subtraction |
|---|---|
| add          plus | subtract          minus |
| sum          more than | difference          less than |
| increased by | decreased by          take away |

| Multiplication | Division |
|---|---|
| times | divided by |
| multiplied by | divided into |
| product | quotient |

**Write an algebraic expression for the difference of a number and 8.**

1. What operation would you choose?   subtraction

2. Write an algebraic expression.   $n - 8$

**Write an algebraic expression for 3 more than a number.**

3. What operation would you choose?   addition

4. Write an algebraic expression.   $n + 3$

**Write an algebraic expression for the quotient of a number and 15.**

5. What operation would you choose?   division

6. Write an algebraic expression.   $n \div 15$

**Write an algebraic expression.**

7. the product of 12 and a number $k$   $12k$

8. a number $d$ increased by 9   $d + 9$

9. a number $h$ divided by 4   $h \div 4$

## Challenge
### 2-8 What's My Equation?

Match each equation with the word problem it represents. Write the equation and corresponding letter. Then write the letter of the equation in the circle that has the problem number. Discover the message formed by the letters.

| **P** $2k = 14$ | **D** $\dfrac{p}{3} = 2.50$ | **A** $\dfrac{m}{5} = 8$ | **U** $3t = 21$ |
|---|---|---|---|
| **M** $a - 18 = 33$ | **S** $w + 7 = 25$ | **T** $x + 7 = 22$ | **H** $n - 12 = 37$ |

1. Tom has 7 more CDs than Rick does. If Tom has 22 CDs, how many does Rick have?   $x + 7 = 22$; T   Ⓜ 2

2. Maria is 18 years younger than Kim. If Maria is 33, how old is Kim?   $a - 18 = 33$; M   Ⓐ 3

3. Five friends went out for dinner. They shared the cost of the meal equally. If each person paid $8, what was the total cost of the meal?   $\dfrac{m}{5} = 8$; A   Ⓣ 1

4. Max paid 3 times as much for a tape as his friend did. If Max paid $21, how much did his friend pay?   $3t = 21$; U   Ⓗ 8

5. Marisa and her two friends share a pizza. The cost of the pizza is shared equally among them. If each person pays $2.50, how much does the pizza cost?   $\dfrac{p}{3} = 2.50$; D   Ⓐ 3   Ⓓ 5

6. Lee has scored twice as many goals as Jiang has. If Lee's goal total is 14, how many goals has Jiang scored?   $2k = 14$; P   Ⓓ 5   Ⓢ 7

7. Jamal sold 7 more magazine subscriptions than Wayne did. If Jamal sold 25 subscriptions, how many did Wayne sell?   $w + 7 = 25$; S   Ⓤ 4

8. Shelly delivered 12 fewer newspapers this week than last week. If she delivered 37 papers this week, how many did she deliver last week?   $n - 12 = 37$; H   Ⓟ 6

## Problem Solving
*Translate Words into Math*

**Write the correct answer.**

**1.** Employers in the United States allocate $n$ fewer vacation days than the 25 days given by the average Japanese employer. Write an expression to show the number of vacation days given U.S. workers.

$25 - n$

**2.** There are 112 members in the Somerset Marching Band. They will march in $r$ equal rows. Write an expression for the number of band members in each row.

$112 \div r$

**3.** A cup of cottage cheese has 26 grams of protein. Write an expression for the amount of protein in $s$ cups of cottage cheese.

$26s$

**4.** Every morning Sasha exercises for 20 minutes. She exercises $k$ minutes every evening. Next week she will double her exercise time at night. Write an expression to show how long Sasha will exercise each day next week.

$20 + 2k$

**Choose the letter for the best answer.**

**5.** One centimeter equals 0.3937 inches. Which expression shows how many inches are in $c$ centimeters?

A $0.3937 + c$

B $0.3937 \div c$

C $c \div 0.3937$

D̲ $0.3937c$

**6.** In 1957, the Soviet Union launched *Sputnik 1*, the first satellite to orbit Earth. It circled Earth's orbit every 1.6 hours for 92 days, then burned up. If the satellite traveled $m$ miles per hour, which expression shows the length of the orbit?

F $92m$

G̲ $1.6m$

H $m \div 1.6$

J $92 \div m$

**7.** Gina's heart rate is 70 beats per minute. Which expression shows the number of beats in $h$ hours?

A $70h$

B $60h$

C̲ $4,200h$

D $3,600h$

**8.** The Harris family went on vacation for $w$ weeks and 3 days. Which expression shows the total number of days of their vacation?

F $7w$

G $3w$

H̲ $7w + 3$

J $3w + 7$

79    **Holt Middle School Math    Course 2**

---

## Puzzles, Twisters & Teasers
*Birds of a Feather!*

Solve the crossword puzzle. Then use the letters in the shaded boxes to answer the riddle. You'll need to use some letters more than once.

**Across**

**1.** something that does not change

**2.** a number or symbol placed to the right of and above another number, symbol, or expression

**6.** putting together

**8.** the letter in a term

**9.** a number, a variable, or a product of numbers and variables

**Down**

**1.** the number in a term

**3.** the multiple expressed by an exponent

**4.** a symbol used for counting

**5.** group similar objects

**7.** similar

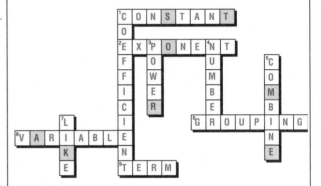

Where do birds invest their money?

In the $\underline{S}\ \underline{T}\ \underline{O}\ \underline{R}\ \underline{K}\ \ \underline{M}\ \underline{A}\ \underline{R}\ \underline{K}\ \underline{E}\ \underline{T}$.

80    **Holt Middle School Math    Course 2**

---

## Exploration Recording Sheet
*Combining Like Terms*

Philipe is organizing the storerooms at an athletic club. He finds **3 cases** and **2 cans** of tennis balls in one room and **5 cases** and **6 cans** of tennis balls in another room. He combines them and has **8 cases** and **8 cans**.

You can represent this situation with algebra tiles and with symbols.

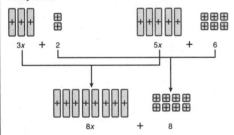

$3x \quad + \quad 2 \qquad\qquad 5x \quad + \quad 6$

$8x \quad + \quad 8$

**Draw algebra tiles to represent each expression, and combine like terms.**

**1.** $4x + 6x$  $10x$

**2.** $5x + 2 + 7x$  $12x + 2$

82    **Holt Middle School Math    Course 2**

---

## Exploration Recording Sheet
*Combining Like Terms (continued)*

**3.** $x + 1 + 2x + 7$  $3x + 8$

**4.** $3x + 4 + 3x + 5$  $6x + 9$

### Think and Discuss

**5. Discuss** your method for combining like terms.

Possible answer: Combine rectangles with rectangles and squares with squares.

**6. Explain** what you could combine when adding $3x + 2 + 5x$.

You can combine $3x$ and $5x$, resulting in the expression $8x + 2$.

83    **Holt Middle School Math    Course 2**

---

**146**    **Holt Middle School Math    Course 2**

## Practice A
### 2-9 Combining Like Terms

**Identify like terms.**

**1.** $6a$  $b$  $a$  $17$  $4b$  $32$  $17a$

$6a$, $a$, and $17a$; $b$ and $4b$; $17$ and $32$

**2.** $x$  $x^2$  $3x$  $3$  $3x^2$  $6$

$x^2$ and $3x^2$; $x$ and $3x$; $3$ and $6$

**3.** $2$  $6z$  $6z^2$  $z$  $17z$  $z^2$  $3$

$6z^2$ and $z^2$; $z$, $6z$, and $17z$; $2$ and $3$

**4.** $m$  $8$  $8m^2$  $8m$  $m^2$  $12m$  $18$

$8m^2$ and $m^2$; $m$, $8m$, and $12m$; $8$ and $18$

**5.** $2p$  $22p$  $56q$  $12^2$  $q$  $34$

$2p$ and $22p$; $56q$ and $q$; $12^2$ and $34$

**6.** $d$  $d^2$  $15d^2$  $2d$  $4^2$  $5d$  $44$

$d$, $2d$, and $5d$; $d^2$ and $15d^2$; $4^2$ and $44$

**Combine like terms.**

**7.** $6p^2 + 3p^2$

$9p^2$

**8.** $9x - 6x$

$3x$

**9.** $a^2 + b^2 + 2a^2 + 5b^2$

$3a^2 + 6b^2$

**10.** $7h^2 + 3 - 2h^2 + 4$

$5h^2 + 7$

**11.** $3x + 3y + x + y + z$

$4x + 4y + z$

**12.** $5b + 5b + 6b^2 - 10 - 3b$

$6b^2 + 7b - 10$

**13.** Find the perimeter of the rectangle. Combine like terms.

**A** $4x + 3y$
**B** $8x + 6y$
**C** $12xy$
**D** $4x^2 + 3y^2$

84  **Holt Middle School Math   Course 2**

---

## Practice B
### 2-9 Combining Like Terms

**Identify like terms.**

**1.** $3a$  $b^2$  $b^3$  $4b^2$  $4$  $5a$

$3a$ and $5a$; $b^2$ and $4b^2$

**2.** $x$  $x^4$  $4x$  $4x^2$  $4x^4$  $3x^2$

$x$ and $4x$; $x^4$ and $4x^4$; $4x^2$ and $3x^2$

**3.** $6m$  $6m^2$  $n^2$  $2n$  $2$  $4m$  $5n$

$6m$ and $4m$; $2n$ and $5n$

**4.** $12s$  $7s^4$  $9s$  $s^2$  $5$  $5s^4$  $2$

$12s$ and $9s$; $7s^4$ and $5s^4$; $5$ and $2$

**Combine like terms.**

**5.** $2p + 22q^2 - p$

$p + 22q^2$

**6.** $x^2 + 3x^2 - 4^2$

$4x^2 - 16$

**7.** $n^4 + n^3 + 3n - n - n^3$

$n^4 + 2n$

**8.** $4a + 4b + 2 - 2a + 5b - 1$

$2a + 9b + 1$

**9.** $32m^2 + 14n^2 - 12m^2 + 5n - 3$

$20m^2 + 14n^2 + 5n - 3$

**10.** $2h^2 + 3g - 2h^2 + 2^2 - 3 + 4g$

$7g + 1$

**11.** Write an expression for the perimeter of the figure at right. Combine like terms in the expression.

$2v + 8s + 5$

**12.** Write an expression for the combined perimeters of the figures at right. Combine like terms in the expression.

$14a + 2b + 4$

85  **Holt Middle School Math   Course 2**

---

## Practice C
### 2-9 Combining Like Terms

**Combine like terms.**

**1.** $8k^2 + 4k - 3k^2 + 3^2 - k + 5$

$5k^2 + 3k + 14$

**2.** $10x^3 + 5y^2 + 2xy - 4y^2 + 4xy - x^3$

$9x^3 + y^2 + 6xy$

**3.** $3a + 2b^2 + 6c + a - 2c + b^2 + c$

$4a + 3b^2 + 5c$

**4.** $12x^4 + 6x^2 + 5x^3 - x^2 + 2xy - 8x^4$

$4x^4 + 5x^3 + 5x^2 + 2xy$

**5.** $9p^6 + q^2 + 6p + 5q^2 + 5p - 5q^2$

$9p^6 + q^2 + 11p$

**6.** $h^2 + 4h + 4h^2 - h + 4 + h^2 + 7h$

$6h^2 + 10h + 4$

**7.** Write an expression that has five terms and simplifies to $5m^3 + 4n$ when you combine like terms.

Possible answer: $3m^3 + 5n + 4m^3 - 2m^3 - n$

**8.** Write an expression for the perimeter of the figure to the right. Combine like terms in the expression.

$6x + 7y + 5$

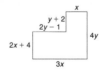

**9.** Write an expression to find the combined perimeters of the figures to the right. Combine like terms in the expression.

$12a + 14b + 12$

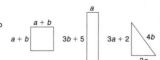

**10.** Jake scored $x$ points in the first basketball game. He scored 2 fewer points in the next game. His teammate, Jack, scored $2y$ points in the first game and 4 more than twice as many points in the next game. Write an expression for the total number of points scored by both players and combine like terms.

$2x + 6y + 2$

86  **Holt Middle School Math   Course 2**

---

## Reteach
### 2-9 Combining Like Terms

Look at the following expressions: $x = 1x$
$$x + x = 2x$$
$$x + x + x = 3x$$
The numbers 1, 2, and 3 are called **coefficients** of $x$.

**Identify each coefficient.**

**1.** $3n$ ___3___   **2.** $7y$ ___7___   **3.** $m$ ___1___   **4.** $9$ ___0___

An algebraic expression has terms that are separated by $+$ and $-$. In the expression $2x + 5y$, the **terms** are $2x$ and $5y$.

| Expression | Terms |
|---|---|
| $8x + 4y$ | $8x$ and $4y$ |
| $m - 3n$ | $m$ and $3n$ |
| $4a^2 - 2b + a$ | $4a^2$, $2b$, and $a$ |
| $6d \div 2p$ | $6d$ and $2p$ |

Sometimes the terms of an expression can be combined. Only **like terms** can be combined.

| $7w + w$ | like terms |
|---|---|
| $2x - 2y + 2$ | unlike terms because $x$ and $y$ are different variables |
| $8e - 3e + 2e$ | like terms |
| $5d + 25g$ | unlike terms because $d$ and $g$ are different variables |

To simplify an expression:
**Step 1:** Combine like terms.
**Step 2:** Add or subtract the coefficients of the variable.

$$7w + w = 8w$$
$$6y + 1 - 3y = 3y + 1$$

**Combine like terms.**

**5.** $y + 5y$

$6y$

**6.** $9x - 4x$

$5x$

**7.** $5s - 2s$

$3s$

**8.** $3d + 7d$

$10d$

**9.** $3b + b + 6$

$4b + 6$

**10.** $8a - a - 3$

$7a - 3$

**11.** $2p + 4p + r$

$6p + r$

**12.** $9b - 8b + c$

$b + c$

87  **Holt Middle School Math   Course 2**

---

## Challenge
### Matching Terms

Draw a line from each set of terms in Column A to its equivalent combination in Column B. Then circle each letter in Column B that does not have a matching term. Unscramble those letters to answer the riddle.

| Column A | Column B |
|---|---|
| 1. $2x + 7 + 5x - 4 - x$ | A. $5y + 9x + 12$ |
| 2. $5 + 7x + 2x - 3 + 6$ | B. $12y + 6x + 24$ |
| 3. $x + y + 4x - 3x + 2y + 3y$ | C. 15 |
| 4. $3x^2 + 5x - 17 + 6x + 20$ | D. $9x + 8$ |
| 5. $4x + x^2 + 12 - 4 + 2x$ | E. 4 |
| 6. $12y + 12x + 12 - 6x + 12$ | F. $6x + 3$ |
| 7. $12y + 4 + x - 7y + 8 + 8x$ | G. $11x + y + 7$ |
| 8. $5x + x^2 + 2x + 5 - 4 - x^2$ | H. $x^2 + 6x + 8$ |
| 9. $5x^2 + 8x + 7x^2 + 6x$ | I. $4x$ |
| 10. $12x + 6 - 8x - 4x - 3 + 12$ | J. $3x^2 + 11x + 3$ |
| 11. $5x + 4 - 3x + 5 + 2x - 9$ | K. $3x + 2$ |
| 12. $4x + 2y + 8 - 3 - y - x$ | L. $3x^2$ |
| 13. $4x + 5 + 7x + 2y + 2 - y$ | M. $6x$ |
| 14. $2y + 2x + 8 - 6 + x - 2y$ | N. $x^2 + 3x$ |
| 15. $4x + 6y + 6 + 7x + y$ | O. $6x^2 + 6y + 1$ |
| 16. $3x^2 + 4x - 2x^2 - 3x + 2x$ | P. $12x^2 + 14x$ |
| 17. $8x + 4 - 4 - 4x + x$ | Q. $7x + 1$ |
| 18. $y + 5x + 6y + 9 - 6$ | R. $x^2$ |
| 19. $x^2 + 3 + 2x^2 + 4 - 7$ | S. $5x + 7y + 3$ |
| 20. $5y + 3 + 7x^2 - 2 - x^2 + y$ | T. 0 |
| | U. $2x + 6y$ |
| | V. $3x + y + 5$ |
| | W. $11x + 7y + 6$ |
| | X. $5x$ |

**Riddle:** What can be a word, a number, a period of time, or a variable?

A _T_ _E_ _R_ _M_

**Holt Middle School Math   Course 2**

---

## Problem Solving
### Combining Like Terms

Write the correct answer. Use the figures for Problems 1–3.

**Figure 1          Figure 2**

1. Figure 1 shows the length of each side of a garden. Write an expression for the perimeter of the garden.

   $2a + 2b + 2c$

2. Figure 2 is a square swimming pool. Write an expression to show the perimeter of the pool.

   $4b$

3. Write an expression for the combined perimeter of the garden and the pool.

   $2a + 6b + 2c$

4. The Pantheon in Rome has $n$ granite columns in each of 3 rows. Write an addition expression to show the number of columns, then combine like terms and evaluate the expression for $n = 8$.

   $n + n + n$; $3n = 24$;

   24 columns

**Choose the letter for the best answer.**

5. Which is an expression that shows the earnings of a telemarketer who worked for 23 hours at a salary of $d$ dollars per hour?

   A $d + 23$     C $d \div 23$
   Ⓑ $23d$     D $23 \div d$

6. The minimum wage in 1997 was $5.15 per hour. Evaluate the expression $40h$ where $h = $5.15$ to find a worker's weekly salary.

   F $20.60     H $515.00
   G $200     Ⓙ $206.00

7. What is the perimeter of a triangle with sides the following lengths: $2a + 4c$, $3c + 7$, and $6a - 4$. Combine like terms in the expression.

   A $8a + 11c$
   B $6a + 7c + 3$
   Ⓒ $8a + 7c + 3$
   D $8a + 7c + 11$

8. A hexagon is a 6-sided figure. Find the perimeter of a hexagon where all of the sides are the same length. The expression $x + y$ represents the length of a side. Combine like terms in the expression.

   Ⓕ $6x + 6y$
   G $6 + x + y$
   H $6x + y$
   J $6xy$

**Holt Middle School Math   Course 2**

---

## Puzzles, Twisters & Teasers
### In Other Words. . .

Write each verbal expression as an algebraic expression. Then use the answer key to solve the riddle.

1. the product of 20 and $t$     $20t$

2. the sum of 4 times a number and 2     $4n + 2$

3. the product of 7 and $p$     $7p$

4. the sum of six times a number and 1     $6n + 1$

5. the sum of 5 and a number     $5 + n$

6. the quotient of a number and 8     $\dfrac{n}{8}$

7. $m$ plus 6     $m + 6$

8. $t$ less than 23     $23 - t$

9. the quotient of 100 and the amount 6 plus $w$     $\dfrac{100}{(6 + w)}$

**Answer Key**

| + | − | × | ÷ |
|---|---|---|---|
| S H L B | N | G A | C I |

What's worse than raining cats and dogs?

H A I L I N G
+ × ÷ + ÷ − ×

C A B S
÷ × + +

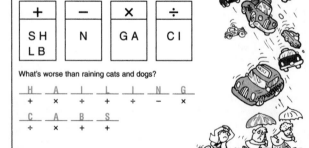

**Holt Middle School Math   Course 2**

---

## Exploration Recording Sheet
### Equations and Their Solutions

Marie spent $2. She has $5 left. How much did she have before she spent the $2?

The equation $x - 2 = 5$ represents the problem.

Because $7 - 2 = 5$ is a true statement, $x = 7$.

The solution to the equation $x - 2 = 5$ is 7, and the answer to the question is $7.

1. Make up three real-world problems that have 7 for an answer.

   Possible answers; a) The cost of $56 was shared. Each paid $8. How many people shared the cost? b) Alice had 3 pieces of cake. Toni gave her more until she had 10. How many pieces did Toni give Alice? c) The room had 3 rows of chairs, and each row had the same number of chairs. If there were 21 chairs in the room, how many chairs were in each row?

2. Write three equations that represent your problems in number 1.

   a. $\dfrac{56}{8} = x$     b. $3 + x = 10$     c. $3x = 21$

**Think and Discuss**

3. **Explain** what a solution to an equation is.

   Possible answer: A solution to an equation is a value that makes the equation true.

4. **Describe** how to determine whether 75 is a solution to the equation $25 = 100 - x$.

   Possible answer: Replace the variable $x$ with the value 75, and determine whether the statement is true. $25 = 100 - 75$ is true, so 75 is the solution to $25 = 100 - x$.

**Holt Middle School Math   Course 2**

---

**Holt Middle School Math   Course 2**

## Practice A
### Equations and Their Solutions

**Tell if each number is a solution of $n + 5 = 27$.**

1. 32      2. 22      3. 21      4. 34

  no      yes      no      no

**Tell if each number is a solution of $19 + a = 40$.**

5. 49      6. 31      7. 21      8. 39

  no      no      yes      no

**Tell if each number is a solution of $72 - x = 50$.**

9. 22      10. 122      11. 28      12. 18

  yes      no      no      no

**Tell if each number is a solution of $5 = 23 - w$.**

13. 28      14. 17      15. 13      16. 18

  no      no      no      yes

17. As of the 2000–2001 NBA season, Coach Phil Jackson had lost 234 games. This number is 434 fewer games than he won. The equation $234 = g - 434$ can be used to show the number of games Coach Jackson has won. Did he win 200, 464, or 668 games?

  668 games

18. Austin paid $350 for a new video game console. This is $125 more than a used console costs. The equation $350 = c + 125$ can be used to show the cost of a used video game console. Does a used console cost $225, $275, or $475?

  $225

19. In the United States, there are 63 endangered species that are mammals. There are 15 more endangered species that are birds. Are there 78 or 48 endangered species of birds in the United States?

  78 endangered species

20. At The Bike and Blade Shop, mountain bikes are on sale for $349. This is $30 more than a racing bike costs. Does the racing bike cost $319 or $379?

  $319

   93    **Holt Middle School Math Course 2**

---

## Practice B
### Equations and Their Solutions

**Determine if each number is a solution of $21 = x - 3$.**

1. 18      2. 26      3. 17      4. 24

  no      no      no      yes

**Determine if each number is a solution of $b + 19 = 52$.**

5. 71      6. 3      7. 33      8. 13

  no      no      yes      no

**Determine if the given numbers are solutions of the given equations.**

9. $k = 24$ for $3k = 6$      10. $m = 3$ for $42 = m + 39$      11. $y = 8$ for $8y + 6 = 70$

  no      yes      yes

12. $s = 5$ for $18 = 3s - 3$      13. $x = 7$ for $23 - k = 30$      14. $v = 12$ for $84 = 7v$

  no      no      yes

15. $c = 15$ for $45 - 2c = 15$         16. $x = 10$ for $x + 25 = 2x + 4 = 19$

  yes         yes

17. $e = 6$ for $42 = 51 - e$         18. $p = 15$ for $19 = p - 4$

  no         no

19. $h = 9$ for $120 - 3h = 97$         20. $a = 25$ for $300 = 500 - 8a$

  no         yes

21. Earth's diameter is about 7,926 miles. This is about 407 miles greater than the diameter of Venus. The equation $7,926 = v + 407$ can be used to represent the length of Venus' diameter. Is the diameter of Venus 8,333 miles or 7,519 miles?

  7,519 miles

22. Jason and Maya have their own Web sites on the Internet. As of last week, Jason's Web site had 2,426 visitors. This is twice as many visitors as Maya had. Did Maya have 1,213 visitors or 4,852 visitors to her Web site?

  1,213 visitors

   94    **Holt Middle School Math Course 2**

---

## Practice C
### Equations and Their Solutions

**Determine if the given numbers are solutions of the given equations.**

1. $a = 15$ for $75 \div a = 5$      2. $x = 90$ for $x \div 9 = 100 - x$

  yes      yes

3. $d = 8$ for $875 = 909 - 4d$      4. $x = 32$ for $2x - 25 + x - 70 = 1$

  no      yes

5. $e = 2$ for $e^3 - e^2 = 6e - 8$      6. $b = 4$ for $b^2 + 2b - 3 = 27$

  yes      no

7. $d = 12$ for $4d - 24 - 12 = 0$      8. $r = 9$ for $4r^2 - 19 - 5r = 340$

  no      no

9. $p = 25$ for $\frac{4p}{5} + 2p + 10 = 80$      10. $t = 18$ for $\frac{t}{6} + \frac{54}{t} = 3$

  yes      no

11. In 1991, there were about 7,200,000 cell phone subscribers in the United States. This is about 120,300,000 fewer subscribers than there were by the year 2001. The equation $7,200,000 = s - 120,300,000$ can be used to represent the number of cell phone subscribers in 2001. Were there 113,100,000 or 127,500,000 cell phone subscribers in the United States in 2001?

  127,500,000 cell phone subscribers

12. Hector bought 50 shares of an Internet stock. He paid a commission of $15. The total cost of the transaction was $150. The equation $150 = 50n + 15$ can be used to represent the price Hector paid for each share of stock. Did he pay $5.70, $3.00, or $2.70 per share of stock?

  $2.70 per share

13. The Super State Car Dealership has 120 mid-sized cars on the lot. There are half as many luxury cars as compact cars. There are 10 more pick-up trucks than luxury cars and half as many compact cars as mid-sized cars. Are there 40, 50, or 60 pick-up trucks on the lot of this car dealership?

  40 pick-up trucks

   95    **Holt Middle School Math Course 2**

---

## Reteach
### Equations and Their Solutions

Number sentences that contain an equal sign (=) are called equations.

Equations may be true, or they may be false.

$3 + 1 = 4$

| True | False |
|---|---|
| $3 + 4 = 7$ | $3 + 1 = 7$ |
| $8 - 6 = 2$ | $8 - 2 = 5$ |

$8 - 2 = 6$

An equation may contain a variable.

  variable →    $x + 4 = 6$

Whether this equation is true or false depends on the value of $x$.

You can decide if a number is a *solution* of an equation. Substitute the number for the variable in the equation. If the equation is a true equation, then the number is the **solution**.

Equation: $x + 4 = 6$

| Is 2 a solution? | Is 3 a solution? |
|---|---|
| $x + 4 = 6$ | $x + 4 = 6$ |
| Substitute 2 for $x$ | Substitute 3 for $x$ |
| $2 + 4 \overset{?}{=} 6$ | $3 + 4 \overset{?}{=} 6$ |
| $6 \overset{?}{=} 6$   True | $7 \overset{?}{=} 6$   False |

2 is a solution of $x + 4 = 6$.    3 is not a solution of $x + 4 = 6$.

**Determine if the number is a solution of the equation.**

1. Is 3 a solution of $y + 3 = 9$?      2. Is 4 a solution of $n + 6 = 10$?

  no      yes

3. Is 2 a solution of $w - 1 = 1$?      4. Is 1 a solution of $x + 50 = 49$?

  yes      no

5. Is 6 a solution of $c + 23 = 30$?      6. Is 9 a solution of $v - 9 = 0$?

  no      yes

7. Is 20 a solution of $t - 17 = 3$?      8. Is 16 a solution of $12 + a = 24$?

  yes      no

9. Is 25 a solution of $38 - m = 13$?      10. Is 8 a solution of $15 = e + 5$?

  yes      no

   96    **Holt Middle School Math Course 2**

---

## Challenge
### *The Solution Is BINGO!*

Find the solution to each problem or equation. Cross it out on the board below to get BINGO!

1. Is 37, 47, or 67 a solution for $52 = n + 15$?

   37

2. Is 14, 17, or 21 a solution for $8y - 7 = 129$?

   17

3. Is 14, 22, or 24 a solution for $132 - (4x - 5) = 81$?

   14

4. Is 12, 15, or 18 a solution for $3(60 - s) - 2s = 105$?

   15

5. Garret scored 18 points in his last basketball game, which is 6 fewer points than Vince scored. The equation $18 = p - 6$ can be used to represent Vince's points. Did Vince score 12, 24, or 28 points?

   24

6. In 3 years, Sarah's sister will be twice as old as Sarah. If Sarah is now 3 years old, will her sister be 6, 9, or 12 years old in 3 years?

   12

7. The highest recorded temperature in Alaska was 100°F in 1915. This was 56 years before the lowest recorded temperature of −80°F. Was the lowest recorded temperature in 1856, 1956, or 1971?

   1971

8. In 1999, Florida had 2,145 elementary schools. This was 288 fewer elementary schools than 3 times the number of elementary schools in South Carolina during the same year. Did South Carolina have 427, 811, or 1,857 elementary schools in 1999?

   811

| B | I | N | G | O |
|---|---|---|---|---|
| ~~17~~ | 67 | 24 | ~~37~~ | ~~1971~~ |
| 6 | ~~24~~ | 47 | 1,857 | 22 |
| 427 | 1956 | FREE | 18 | ~~14~~ |
| ~~12~~ | 9 | 16 | ~~811~~ | 1856 |
| 28 | 23 | 21 | 19 | ~~15~~ |

---

## Problem Solving
### *Equations and Their Solutions*

Write the correct answer.

1. The jet airplane was invented in 1939. This is 12 years after the first television was invented. Was television invented in 1927 or 1951?

   1927

2. There are three times as many students in the high school as in the junior high school, which has 330 students. Does the high school have 990 students or 110 students?

   990 students

3. The frigate bird has been recorded at speeds up to 95 mi/h. The only faster bird ever recorded was the spine-tailed swift at 11 mi/h faster. Was the speed of the spine-tailed swift 84 mi/h or 106 mi/h?

   106 mi/h

4. As of February 2000, 14.6 million households in Canada were online. This is 10.1 million more households online than in Australia. Were 24.7 million or 4.5 million households online in Australia?

   4.5 million

Choose the letter for the best answer.

5. In the United States, the average school year is 180 days. This is 71 days less than the average school year in China. What is the average school year in China?

   Ⓐ 251 days
   B 109 days
   C 151 days
   D 271 days

6. The longest bridge in the world is the Akashi Kaikyo Bridge in Japan. Its main span is 1,290 feet longer than a mile. A mile is 5,280 feet. How long is the Akashi Kaikyo bridge?

   F 3,990 feet
   G 6,400 feet
   H 4,049 feet
   Ⓙ 6,570 feet

7. *Ornithomimus* stood about 6 feet tall and was the fastest dinosaur at a speed of about 50 mi/h. The largest dinosaur, *Seismosaurus*, was 20 times as tall. How tall was *Seismosaurus*?

   A 12 feet
   B 70 feet
   Ⓒ 120 feet
   D 26 feet

8. Milton collects sports trading cards. He has 80 baseball cards. He has half as many basketball cards as football cards. He has 20 more hockey cards than basketball cards and half as many football cards as baseball cards. How many hockey cards does he have?

   F 20 hockey cards
   Ⓖ 40 hockey cards
   H 60 hockey cards
   J 80 hockey cards

---

## Puzzles, Twisters & Teasers
### *The Answer Popped Right into My Head!*

Find the solution for each equation below. Write the letter on the line above the correct answer at the bottom of the page to solve the riddle.

P  $18 = s - 7$   25
M  $x + 3 = 10$   7
O  $12 = t + 9$   3
Y  $s - 38 = 57$   95
R  $16 - j = 12$   4
I  $16 = 34 - m$   18
U  $48 = x + 12$   36
S  $17 + k = 40$   23
N  $24 = 34 - n$   10
B  $p + 18 = 29$   11
A  $47 = v - 6$   53
G  $94 = c + 6$   88
H  $82 = j + 9$   73
E  $a - 15 = 17$   32
T  $15 = k - 9$   24

What did one firecracker say to the other?

| M | Y | | P | O | P | | I | S |
|---|---|---|---|---|---|---|---|---|
| 7 | 95 | | 25 | 3 | 25 | | 18 | 23 |

| B | I | G | G | E | R | | T | H | A | N |
|---|---|---|---|---|---|---|---|---|---|---|
| 11 | 18 | 88 | 88 | 32 | 4 | | 24 | 73 | 53 | 10 |

| Y | O | | U | R | | P | O | P |
|---|---|---|---|---|---|---|---|---|
| 95 | 3 | | 36 | 4 | | 25 | 3 | 25 |

---

## Exploration Recording Sheet
### *Solving Equations by Adding or Subtracting*

Find a solution to each equation.

Equations with Addition

1. $n + 100 = 135$

   $n = $ 35

2. $10 + n = 91$

   $n = $ 81

3. $n + 25 = 75$

   $n = $ 50

4. $13 + n = 23$

   $n = $ 10

Equations with Subtraction

5. $91 - n = 10$

   $n = $ 81

6. $n - 10 = 43$

   $n = $ 53

7. $75 - n = 25$

   $n = $ 50

8. $n - 15 = 23$

   $n = $ 38

**Think and Discuss**

9. **Discuss** your strategies for solving the equations.

   Possible answer: Work backwards using the inverse of the operation shown in the equation.

10. **Describe** how the operations of addition and subtraction "undo" each other.

   Possible answer: Adding 5 and then subtracting 5 is the same as adding or subtracting zero.

---

## Practice A
### Solving Equations by Adding or Subtracting

Match each equation in Column A with its correct solution in Column B.

| Column A | Column B | | Column A | Column B |
|---|---|---|---|---|
| **1.** $n - 16 = 8$ | **A.** $n = 12$ | | **10.** $x - 12 = 13$ | **L.** $x = 14$ |
| **2.** $5 = n - 7$ | **B.** $n = 13$ | | **11.** $x + 8 = 40$ | **M.** $x = 17$ |
| **3.** $12 + n = 25$ | **C.** $n = 17$ | | **12.** $34 = 16 + x$ | **N.** $x = 18$ |
| **4.** $n - 17 = 11$ | **D.** $n = 24$ | | **13.** $x + 5 = 19$ | **P.** $x = 25$ |
| **5.** $n + 18 = 35$ | **E.** $n = 27$ | | **14.** $4 + x = 52$ | **Q.** $x = 32$ |
| **6.** $7 = n - 28$ | **F.** $n = 28$ | | **15.** $12 + x = 50$ | **R.** $x = 33$ |
| **7.** $n - 12 = 40$ | **G.** $n = 35$ | | **16.** $15 = x - 2$ | **S.** $x = 38$ |
| **8.** $24 = n - 25$ | **H.** $n = 49$ | | **17.** $52 = x + 9$ | **T.** $x = 43$ |
| **9.** $46 = n + 19$ | **J.** $n = 52$ | | **18.** $x - 11 = 22$ | **U.** $x = 48$ |

**19.** Chris has 55 baseball trading cards. He has 17 more cards than his sister Sara has. Write and solve an equation to find how many trading cards Sara has.

$55 = 17 + n; n = 38$

**20.** In 2000, Sammy Sosa hit 50 home runs. His home run total was 23 runs fewer than the number of home runs that Barry Bonds hit the next year. Write and solve an equation to find how many home runs Barry Bonds hit in 2001.

$50 = h - 23; h = 73$

102    Holt Middle School Math   Course 2

---

## Practice B
### Solving Equations by Adding or Subtracting

Solve the equation. Check your answer.

**1.** $33 = y - 44$     **2.** $r - 32 = 77$     **3.** $125 = x - 29$

$y = 77$       $r = 109$       $x = 154$

**4.** $k + 18 = 25$     **5.** $589 + x = 700$     **6.** $96 = 56 + t$

$k = 7$       $x = 111$       $t = 40$

**7.** $a - 9 = 57$     **8.** $b - 49 = 254$     **9.** $987 = f - 11$

$a = 66$       $b = 303$       $f = 998$

**10.** $32 + d = 1,400$     **11.** $w - 24 = 90$     **12.** $95 = g - 340$

$d = 1,368$       $w = 114$       $g = 435$

**13.** $e - 35 = 59$     **14.** $84 = v + 30$     **15.** $h + 15 = 81$

$e = 94$       $v = 54$       $h = 66$

**16.** $110 = a + 25$     **17.** $45 + c = 91$     **18.** $p - 29 = 78$

$a = 85$       $c = 46$       $p = 107$

**19.** $56 - r = 8$     **20.** $39 = z + 8$     **21.** $93 + g = 117$

$r = 48$       $z = 31$       $g = 24$

**22.** The Morales family is driving from Philadelphia to Boston. So far, they have driven 167 miles. This is 129 miles less than the total distance they must travel. How many miles is Philadelphia from Boston?

The total distance is 296 miles.

**23.** Ron has $1,230 in his savings account. This is $400 more than he needs to buy a new big screen TV. Write and solve an equation to find out how much the TV costs.

$1,230 = t + 400$; The TV costs $830.

103    Holt Middle School Math   Course 2

---

## Practice C
### Solving Equations by Adding or Subtracting

Solve the equation. Check your answer.

**1.** $b - 32 = 15$     **2.** $e - 43 = 121$     **3.** $601 = x - 24$

$b = 47$       $e = 164$       $x = 625$

**4.** $m + 45 = 123$     **5.** $314 + z = 350$     **6.** $840 = 45 + f$

$m = 78$       $z = 36$       $f = 795$

**7.** $d - 67 = 23$     **8.** $w + 233 = 319$     **9.** $91 = x + 52$

$d = 90$       $w = 86$       $x = 39$

**10.** $150 + y = 879$     **11.** $k - 32 = 217$     **12.** $408 = s - 129$

$y = 729$       $x = 249$       $s = 537$

**13.** $108 = j - 24$     **14.** $1,204 = w + 389$     **15.** $p - 167 = 321$

$j = 132$       $w = 815$       $p = 488$

**16.** In 2000, the *Wall Street Journal* was the leading U.S. daily newspaper, with a circulation of 1,762,751. This was 70,085 more than the second leading daily newspaper, *USA Today*. Write and solve an equation to find the circulation of *USA Today* in 2000.

$1,762,751 = c + 70,085$; $c = 1,692,666$

**17.** Mrs. Baker's class has been raising money for a local charity. At the end of last week, they had collected $238. By the end of this week, they had a total of $419. Write and solve an equation to find the amount collected this week.

$238 + m = $419$; $m = $181$

**18.** Andy Green broke the sound barrier on land on October 15, 1997, in Black Rock Desert, Nevada. The speed of sound was recorded at about 751 mi/h. This was about 12 mi/h less than the land speed record that he set that day. Write and solve an equation to find Andy Green's land speed record.

$751 = r - 12$; $r = 763$ mi/h

104    Holt Middle School Math   Course 2

---

## Reteach
### Solving Equations by Adding or Subtracting

Solving an equation is like balancing a scale. If you add the same weight to both sides of a balanced scale, the scale will remain balanced. You can use this same idea to solve an equation.

Think of the equation $x - 7 = 12$ as a balanced scale. The equal sign keeps the balance.

$$x - 7 = 12$$
$\boxed{-7 + 7 = 0}$   $x - 7 + 7 = 12 + 7$   Add 7 to both sides.
$$x + 0 = 19$$    Combine like terms.
$$x = 19$$

When you solve an equation, the idea is to get the variable by itself. What you do to one side of the equation, you must do to the other side.

• To solve a subtraction equation, use addition.
• To solve an addition equation, use subtraction.

Solve and check: $y + 8 = 14$.

$$y + 8 = 14$$
$\boxed{+8 - 8 = 0}$   $y + 8 - 8 = 14 - 8$   Subtract 8 from both sides.
$$y + 0 = 6$$    Combine like terms.
$$y = 6$$

**Check:**   $y + 8 = 14$    To check, substitute 6 for $y$.
$$6 + 8 \overset{?}{=} 14$$
$$14 \overset{?}{=} 14 \checkmark$$

A true sentence, $14 = 14$, means the solution is correct.

Solve and check.

**1.** $x - 2 = 8$          **2.** $b + 5 = 11$

$x - 2 + 2 = 8 + 2$     $b + 5 - 5 = 11 - 5$

$x - 0 = 10$         $b + 0 = 6$

**3.** $n + 8 = 11$   **4.** $y - 6 = 2$   **5.** $a - 9 = 4$   **6.** $m + 2 = 18$

$n = 3$     $y = 8$     $a = 13$     $m = 16$

105    Holt Middle School Math   Course 2

---

Use each term once to make up one addition and one subtraction equation, then solve the equations. Possible answers given.

**1.** m, n, 12, 6, 54, 9

$n - 12 = 54; n = 66$

$m + 6 = 9; m = 3$

**2.** x, y, 7, 15, 32, 45

$x - 15 = 32; x = 47$

$y + 7 = 45; y = 38$

**3.** p, q, 19, 44, 72, 8

$p + 19 = 72; p = 53$

$q - 8 = 44; q = 52$

**4.** a, b, 67, 102, 6, 8

$a - 102 = 6; a = 108$

$b + 8 = 67; b = 59$

**5.** c, d, 11, 12, 18, 35

$c - 18 = 35; c = 53$

$d + 11 = 12; d = 1$

**6.** s, t, 115, 123, 32, 0

$s + 115 = 123; s = 8$

$t - 32 = 0; t = 32$

**7.** w, y, 1, 2, 3, 4

$w - 2 = 1; w = 3$

$y + 3 = 4; y = 1$

**8.** n, p, 6, 22, 99, 400

$n - 6 = 400; n = 406$

$p + 22 = 99; p = 77$

**9.** e, f, 52, 4, 75, 18

$e + 4 = 75; e = 71$

$f - 18 = 52; f = 70$

**10.** g, h, 61, 88, 94, 117

$g - 117 = 61; g = 178$

$h + 88 = 94; h = 6$

**11.** k, l, 302, 54, 115, 79

$k - 54 = 115; k = 169$

$l + 79 = 302; l = 223$

**12.** r, s, 90, 14, 71, 15

$r + 15 = 90; r = 75$

$s - 14 = 71; s = 85$

**13.** u, v, 8, 12, 37, 44

$u - 37 = 44; u = 81$

$v + 8 = 12; v = 4$

**14.** x, y, 198, 0, 231, 4

$x - 198 = 4; x = 202$

$y + 0 = 231; y = 231$

Holt Middle School Math Course 2

---

Write the correct answer.

**1.** In an online poll, 1,927 people voted for Coach as the best job at the Super Bowl. The job of Announcer received 8,055 more votes. Write and solve an equation to find how many votes the job of Announcer received.

$1,927 = v - 8,055; v = 9,982;$
9,982 votes

**2.** In 2001, the largest bank in the world was Mizuho Holdings, Japan, with $1,295 billion in assets. This was $351 billion more than the largest bank in the United States, Citigroup. Write and solve an equation to find Citigroup's assets.

$1,295 = a + 351; a = 944;$
$944 billion

**3.** The two smallest countries in the world are Vatican City and Monaco. Vatican City is 1.37 square kilometers smaller than Monaco, which is 1.81 square kilometers in area. What is the area of Vatican City?

0.44 square km

**4.** The Library of Congress is the largest library in the world. It has 24 million books, which is 8 million more than the National Library of Canada has. How many books does the National Library of Canada have?

16 million books

Choose the letter for the best answer.

**5.** The first track on Sean's new CD has been playing for 55 seconds. This is 42 seconds less than the time of the entire first track. How long is the first track on this CD?

A 37 seconds    C 97 seconds
B 63 seconds    D 93 seconds

**6.** There are 45 students on the school football team. This is 13 more than the number of students on the basketball team. How many students are on the basketball team?

F 58 students    H 32 students
G 48 students    J 42 students

**7.** A used mountain bike costs $79.95. This is $120 less than the cost of a new one. If c is the cost of the new bike, which equation can you use to find the cost of a new bike?

A $79.95 = c + 120$
B $120 = 79.95 - c$
C $79.95 = c - 120$
D $120 = 79.95 + c$

**8.** The goal of the School Bake Sale is to raise $125 more than last year's sale. Last year the Bake Sale raised $320. If it reaches its goal, how much will the Bake Sale raise this year?

F $445
G $195
H $525
J $425

Holt Middle School Math Course 2

---

Find the solution for each equation below. Write the letter of each variable on the line above the correct answer at the bottom of the page to solve the riddle.

**1.** $y - 35 = 17$     $y = 52$

**2.** $h - 40 = 26$    $h = 66$

**3.** $a + 16 = 43$    $a = 27$

**4.** $110 = e + 66$   $e = 44$

**5.** $97 = w - 44$    $w = 141$

**6.** $n - 8 = 3$      $n = 11$

**7.** $356 = g - 218$  $g = 574$

**8.** $652 + t = 800$  $t = 148$

**9.** $16 = a - 124$   $a = 27$

**10.** $63 + m = 903$  $m = 840$

**11.** $k + 18 = 98$   $k = 80$

**12.** $d - 27 = 54$   $d = 81$

**13.** $c - 50 = 23$   $c = 73$

**14.** $l - 62 = 937$  $l = 999$

Why did the robber take a shower?

| H | E | | W | A | N | T | E | D | | T | O |
|---|---|---|---|---|---|---|---|---|---|---|---|
| 66 | 44 | | 141 | 27 | 11 | 148 | 44 | 81 | | 148 | 140 |

| M | A | K | E | | A | | C | L | E | A | N |
|---|---|---|---|---|---|---|---|---|---|---|---|
| 840 | 27 | 80 | 44 | | 27 | | 73 | 999 | 44 | 27 | 11 |

| G | E | T | | A | W | A | Y |
|---|---|---|---|---|---|---|---|
| 574 | 44 | 148 | | 27 | 141 | 27 | 52 |

Holt Middle School Math Course 2

---

Find a solution to each equation.

Equations with Multiplication

**1.** $n \cdot 4 = 56$

$n = 14$

**2.** $13 \cdot n = 65$

$n = 5$

**3.** $n \cdot 15 = 75$

$n = 5$

**4.** $25 \cdot n = 525$

$n = 21$

Equations with Division

**5.** $n \div 5 = 100$

$n = 500$

**6.** $75 \div n = 15$

$n = 5$

**7.** $n \div 2 = 75$

$n = 150$

**8.** $125 \div n = 25$

$n = 5$

**Think and Discuss**

**9. Discuss** your strategies for solving the equations.

Possible answer: Work backwards using the inverse of the operation shown in the equation.

**10. Describe** how the operations of multiplication and division "undo" each other.

Possible answer: Multiply 5 and then, dividing by 5 is the same as multiplying or dividing by 1.

Holt Middle School Math Course 2

**Holt Middle School Math   Course 2**

# Solving Equations by Multiplying or Dividing

Solve.

1. $16 = n \div 2$

$n = 32$

2. $\frac{e}{10} = 8$

$e = 80$

3. $25 = \frac{x}{6}$

$x = 150$

4. $18 = \frac{d}{3}$

$d = 54$

5. $a \div 12 = 7$

$a = 84$

6. $30 = b \div 4$

$b = 120$

Solve and check.

7. $7w = 49$

$w = 7$

8. $75 = 3x$

$x = 25$

9. $60 = 12p$

$p = 5$

10. $77 = 11m$

$m = 7$

11. $4h = 48$

$h = 12$

12. $9y = 54$

$y = 6$

13. $2x = 30$

$x = 15$

14. $45 = 5s$

$s = 9$

15. $6z = 42$

$z = 7$

16. The Fruit Stand charges $0.50 each for navel oranges. Kareem paid $4.00 for a large bag of navel oranges. How many did he buy?

8 oranges

17. Jenny can type at a speed of 80 words per minute. It took her 20 minutes to type a report. How many words was the report?

1,600 words

18. At the local gas station, regular unleaded gasoline is priced at $1.10 per gallon. If it cost $16.50 to fill a car's gas tank, how many gallons of gasoline did the tank hold?

15 gallons of gasoline

# Solving Equations by Multiplying or Dividing

Solve the equation.

1. $68 = \frac{r}{4}$

$r = 272$

2. $k \div 24 = 85$

$k = 2,040$

3. $255 = \frac{x}{4}$

$x = 1,020$

4. $42 = w \div 18$

$w = 756$

5. $\frac{a}{15} = 22$

$a = 330$

6. $82 = b \div 5$

$b = 410$

7. $\frac{c}{7} = 9$

$c = 63$

8. $28 = z \div 3$

$z = 84$

9. $\frac{y}{12} = 10$

$y = 120$

Solve the equation. Check the answer.

10. $52w = 364$

$w = 7$

11. $41x = 492$

$x = 12$

12. $410 = 82p$

$p = 5$

13. $35d = 735$

$d = 21$

14. $195 = 65h$

$h = 3$

15. $4k = 140$

$k = 35$

16. $110 = 5e$

$e = 22$

17. $27a = 216$

$a = 8$

18. $96 = 12n$

$n = 8$

19. Ashley earns $5.50 per hour babysitting. She wants to buy a CD player that costs $71.50, including tax. How many hours will she need to work to earn the money for the CD player?

13 hours

20. A cat can jump the height of up to 5 times the length of its tail. Write and solve an equation to show the height a cat can jump if its tail is 13 inches long.

$\frac{h}{5} = 13$; $h = 65$ inches

# Solving Equations by Multiplying or Dividing

Solve the equation. Check the answer.

1. $765 = \frac{n}{12}$

$n = 9,180$

2. $\frac{m}{9} = 26$

$m = 234$

3. $\frac{a}{12} = 14$

$a = 168$

4. $3g = 165$

$g = 55$

5. $308 = 44b$

$b = 7$

6. $27e = 405$

$e = 15$

Translate the sentence into an equation. Then solve the equation.

7. The product of a number $w$ and 145 is 725. $\quad 145w = 725; w = 5$

8. The quotient of a number $f$ and 21 is 14. $\quad f \div 21 = 14; f = 294$

9. A number $b$ times 23 equals 253. $\quad 23b = 253; b = 11$

10. A number $k$ divided by 15 equals 47. $\quad k \div 15 = 47; k = 705$

11. A number $n$ multiplied by 12 is 84. $\quad 12n = 84; n = 7$

12. Ten divided into a number $m$ equals 54. $\quad m \div 10 = 54; m = 540$

13. About three tons of ore must be mined and processed to produce a single ounce of gold. How many tons of ore are required to produce a pound of gold?

48 tons of ore

14. It costs about $2,931 per hour to operate a Boeing 757 airplane. Find the cost to operate a Boeing 757 during a 5-hour flight.

$14,655

15. Each person in the United States eats an average of 23 quarts of ice cream per year. At this rate, Ms. Diamond's seventh-grade class will eat about 1,794 quarts of ice cream this year. How many students are in Ms. Diamond's seventh-grade class?

78 students

16. Jumbo shrimp sell for $14.99 per pound in a local supermarket. One customer spent $74.95 on shrimp for a dinner party. How much shrimp did this customer purchase for the party?

5 pounds

# Solving Equations by Multiplying or Dividing

When you solve an equation, you must get the variable by itself. Remember, what you do to one side of an equation, you must do to the other side.

• To solve a division equation, multiply both sides of the equation by the same number.

Solve and check: $\frac{a}{3} = 4$.

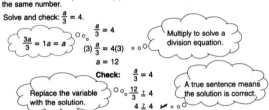

$\frac{3a}{3} = 1a = a$

$\frac{a}{3} = 4$

Multiply to solve a division equation.

$(3)\frac{a}{3} = 4(3)$

$a = 12$

**Check:** $\frac{a}{3} = 4$

Replace the variable with the solution.

$\frac{12}{3} \stackrel{?}{=} 4$

A true sentence means the solution is correct.

$4 \stackrel{?}{=} 4$ ✔

Solve and check.

1. $\frac{x}{6} = 3$

$x = 18$

2. $\frac{s}{8} = 8$

$s = 64$

3. $\frac{c}{10} = 7$

$c = 70$

4. $\frac{n}{3} = 12$

$n = 36$

• To solve a multiplication equation, divide both sides of the equation by the same number.

Solve and check: $5k = 30$.

$\frac{5k}{5} = 1k = k$

$5k = 30$

$\frac{5k}{5} = \frac{30}{5}$

$k = 6$

Divide to solve a multiplication equation.

**Check:** $5k = 30$

$5(6) \stackrel{?}{=} 30$

$30 \stackrel{?}{=} 30$ ✔

True

Replace the variable with the solution.

Solve and check.

5. $2w = 16$

$w = 8$

6. $4b = 24$

$b = 6$

7. $9z = 45$

$z = 5$

8. $10m = 40$

$m = 4$

Find the value of each shape in Exercises 1–8. Then use the values to answer the questions below.

1.
$2 \times \text{butterfly} = 32$
$4 \times \text{butterfly} = \text{bee}$
$\text{butterfly} = \underline{16}; \text{bee} = \underline{4}$

2.
$3 \times \text{drum} = 18$
$2 \times \text{drum} = \text{can}$
$\text{drum} = \underline{6}; \text{can} = \underline{3}$

3.
$4 \times \text{sun} = 8$
$2 \times \text{kite} = \text{sun}$
$\text{sun} = \underline{2}; \text{kite} = \underline{1}$

4.
$12 \times \text{star} = 108$
$3 \times \text{moon} = \text{star}$
$\text{star} = \underline{9}; \text{moon} = \underline{3}$

5.
$24 \times \text{shell1} = 192$
$32 \times \text{shell2} = 0$
$\text{shell1} = \underline{8}; \text{shell2} = \underline{0}$

6.
$39 \times \text{flower} = 117$
$3 \times \text{leaf} = \text{flower}$
$\text{flower} = \underline{3}; \text{leaf} = \underline{1}$

7.
$4 \times \text{banana} = \text{pear} + \text{apple}$
$\text{apple} = \text{pear} + \text{cherry}$
$2 \times \text{banana} = 30$
$\text{banana} = \underline{15}; \text{apple} = \underline{6}; \text{cherry} = \underline{9}$

8.
$2 \times \text{oval} = \text{triangle}$
$5 \times \text{oval} = \text{oval} + \text{triangle}$
$3 \times \text{oval} = 15$
$\text{oval} = \underline{5}; \text{triangle} = \underline{10}; \text{hexagon} = \underline{3}$

9. What was the population of the United States in 1610?

3  5  0

10. What was the population of the United States in 2000?

2  8  1,  4  2  1,  9  0  6

---

Write the correct answer.

1. The Panama Canal cost $387,000,000 to build. Each ship pays $34,000 to pass through the canal. How many ships had to pass through the canal to pay for the cost to build it?

__11,383 ships__

2. The rate of exchange for currency changes daily. One day you could get $25 for 3,302.75 Japanese yen. Write and solve a multiplication equation to find the number of yen per dollar on that day.

$\underline{25y = 3{,}302.75; \ y = 132.11;}$
__132.11 yen per dollar__

3. Franklin D. Roosevelt was in office as president for 12 years. This is three times as long as Jimmy Carter was president. Write and solve an equation to show how long Jimmy Carter was president.

$\underline{12 = 3y; \ y = 4; \ 4 \text{ years}}$

4. The mileage from Dallas to Miami is 1,332 miles. To the nearest hour, how many hours would it take to drive from Dallas to Miami at an average speed of 55 mi/h?

__24 hours__

Choose the letter for the best answer.

5. The total bill for a bike rental for 8 hours was $38. How much per hour was the rental cost?
   A  $8 per hour
   B  $4.75 per hour
   C  $30 per hour
   D  $5.25 per hour

6. If a salesclerk earns $5.75 per hour, how many hours per week does she work to earn her weekly salary of $207?
   F  30 hours
   G  32 hours
   H  36 hours
   J  4 hours

7. At a cost of $0.07 per minute, which equation could you use to find out how many minutes you can talk for $3.15?
   A  $\$0.07 \div m = \$3.15$
   B  $\$3.15 \cdot m = \$0.07$
   C  $\$0.07m = \$3.15$
   D  $\$0.07 \div \$3.15 = m$

8. Which equation shows how to find a runner's distance if he ran a total of $m$ miles in 36 minutes at an average of a mile every 7.2 minutes?
   F  $36 \div m = 7.2$
   G  $7.2 \div m = 36$
   H  $36m = 7.2$
   J  $7.2 \div 36 = m$

---

Find the solution for each equation below. Write the letter of each variable on the line above the correct answer at the bottom of the page to solve the riddle.

1. $a \div 25 = 4$   $a = 100$
2. $w \times 18 = 18$   $w = 1$
3. $r \div 8 = 5$   $r = 40$
4. $3h = 96$   $h = 32$
5. $72 = 8d$   $d = 9$
6. $12 = y \div 4$   $y = 48$
7. $17 = n \div 8$   $n = 136$
8. $85 = 17o$   $o = 5$
9. $3e = 63$   $e = 21$
10. $9 = u \div 3$   $u = 27$
11. $6b = 222$   $b = 37$
12. $7m = 84$   $m = 12$
13. $150 = 3t$   $t = 50$
14. $9s = 99$   $s = 11$

Patient: Doctor! Doctor! I feel like an umbrella!

Doctor:
W  H  Y ,     Y  O  U
1  32  48     48  5  27

M  U  S  T     B  E
12  11  50     37  21

U  N  D  E  R     T  H  E
27  136  9  21  40     50  32  21

W  E  A  T  H  E  R
1  21  100  50  32  21  40

---

**2-1 Exponents** (pp. 60–63)
Find each value.
1. $7^3$ __343__
2. $4^5$ __1,024__
3. $6^4$ __1,296__

Write each number using an exponent and the given base.
4. 64, base 8 __$8^2$__
5. 125, base 5 __$5^3$__
6. 900, base 30 __$30^2$__

**2-2 Powers of Ten and Scientific Notation** (pp. 64–67)
Find each product.
7. $42 \times 10^3$ __42,000__
8. $17 \times 10^1$ __170__
9. $26.7 \times 10^4$ __267,000__

Write each number in scientific notation.
10. 42,600,000 __$4.26 \times 10^7$__
11. 43,000 __$4.3 \times 10^4$__

**2-3 Order of Operations** (pp. 70–74)
Evaluate.
12. $42 - 5 \times 4 + 3$  __25__
13. $5 \times 7 - 18 \div 3$  __29__
14. $5 + (28 \div 7)^2 \div 2$  __13__

15. To raise money for charity, Leslie got pledges from her family. For the first 10 miles that she bikes, she will receive $15, then 50 cents for every mile that she completes after that. If she bikes 32 miles, how much money should she collect?

__$26__

16. Ben spent $6 per square foot for tile for a counter top and $32 for glue and grout. Evaluate the expression $6(24 \times 60) \div 12^2 + \$32$ to find out how much he spent to tile a 24 in. by 60 in. counter top for a kitchen.

__$92__

**2-4 Prime Factorization** (pp. 78–81)
Use a factor tree to find the prime factorization.
17. 12 __$2 \cdot 2 \cdot 3$ or $2^2 \cdot 3$__
18. 42 __$2 \cdot 3 \cdot 7$__

Use a step diagram to prime factor.
19. 196
__$2 \cdot 2 \cdot 7 \cdot 7$ or $2^2 \cdot 7^2$__
20. 320
__$5 \cdot 2 \cdot 2 \cdot 2 \cdot 2 \cdot 2 \cdot 2$ or $5 \cdot 2^6$__

## 2-5 Greatest Common Factor (pp. 82–85)
Find the greatest common factor (GCF).

21. 35, 135 ___5___ 22. 12, 48 ___12___ 23. 16, 24, 64 ___8___

24. A hospital auxiliary is making identical get-well vases of flowers for their patients. They have 128 carnations and 96 roses. What is the greatest number of vases they can fill using all of the flowers?

___32 vases___

## 2-6 Least Common Multiple (pp. 86–90)
Find the least common multiple (LCM).

25. 4, 18 ___36___ 26. 8, 14 ___56___ 27. 5, 13, 20, 26 ___260___

28. A band is practicing for a competition. In the song, a xylophone player plays every fifth beat, and the drummer strikes his drum every sixth beat. When will the xylophone and the drum play the same beat?

___30th beat___

## 2-7 Variables and Algebraic Expressions (pp. 92–95)
Evaluate $n + 12$ for each value of $n$.

29. $n = 4$ ___16___ 30. $n = 12$ ___24___ 31. $n = 6$ ___18___

Evaluate each algebraic expression for the given variables.

32. $6x^2 + 2x + 1$ for $x = 2$ ___29___ 33. $3a + 8a - 9$ for $a = 4$ ___35___

## 2-8 Translate Words Into Math (pp. 96–99)
Write as an algebraic expression.

34. 3 less than the product of 9 and a number ___$9x - 3$___

35. the sum of 6 times a number and 3 ___$6n + 3$___

## 2-9 Combining Like Terms (pp. 100–103)
Combine the like terms.

36. $6a + 4b + 9a$
___$15a + 4b$___

37. $2a + 2b + 3a + 4b + 7$
___$5a + 6b + 7$___

38. $11 + 9x^2 + x + 4$
___$9x^2 + x + 15$___

39. $4a + 6b - 3a + b + 1$
___$a + 7b + 1$___

## 2-10 Equations and Their Solutions (pp. 104–107)
Determine if each number is a solution of $n - 6 = 28$.

40. $n = 42$ ___no___ 41. $n = 34$ ___yes___ 42. $n = 22$ ___no___

43. Jeremy has saved $234 to buy a DVD player, which is $29 less than he needs. Does the DVD player cost $263 or $205?

___$263___

44. Brenda and Cindy are making necklaces. Brenda has 36 beads. This is 8 more than Cindy. The equation $36 = x + 8$ can be used to represent the total number of beads. Does Cindy have 44, 25, or 28 beads?

___28___

## 2-11 Solving Equations by Adding or Subtracting (pp. 110–113)
Solve each equation.

45. $109 = x + 27$
___$x = 82$___

46. $y - 38 = 87$
___$y = 125$___

47. $a + 17 = 50$
___$a = 33$___

48. Robin is reading a 310 page book. She has read 275 pages so far. How many pages does she have yet to read?

___35___

## 2-12 Solving Equations by Multiplying or Dividing (pp. 114–117)
Solve each equation. Check your solution.

49. $\frac{n}{16} = 9$
___$n = 144$___

50. $23x = 115$
___$x = 5$___

51. $15 = y \div 3$
___$y = 45$___

52. Darren wants to buy a new lawn mower for his business. If the mower costs $350 and he can save $50 per week, how many weeks will it take Darren to save the money for the mower?

___7 weeks___

**Space Spaces**

Use the table to construct a model that demonstrates the distances from the Sun to the planets, nearest star, and nearest galaxy.

**Tip:** One benefit of using exponents is that it makes it easier to compare numbers. For example:
Compare $1 \times 10^6$ and $1 \times 10^7$.
Convert $1 \times 10^7$ to $10 \times 10^6$.
$1 \times 10^7$ is ten times as large as $1 \times 10^6$.

Complete the table to express all the distances using a common exponent.

| Object | Average Distance from the Sun (km) | Average Distance from the Sun Expressed with a Common Exponent (km) |
|---|---|---|
| Mercury | $5.80 \times 10^7$ | $5.80 \times 10^7$ |
| Venus | $1.082 \times 10^8$ | $10.82 \times 10^7$ |
| Earth | $1.495 \times 10^8$ | $14.95 \times 10^7$ |
| Mars | $2.279 \times 10^8$ | $22.79 \times 10^7$ |
| Jupiter | $7.780 \times 10^8$ | $77.80 \times 10^7$ |
| Saturn | $1.43 \times 10^9$ | $143 \times 10^7$ |
| Uranus | $2.90 \times 10^9$ | $290 \times 10^7$ |
| Neptune | $4.40 \times 10^9$ | $440 \times 10^7$ |
| Pluto | $5.80 \times 10^9$ | $580 \times 10^7$ |
| Nearest Star | $3.973 \times 10^{13}$ | $3,973,000 \times 10^7$ |
| Nearest Galaxy | $1.514 \times 10^{18}$ | $151,400,000,000 \times 10^7$ |

What problems did you have with your model or drawing? Was it possible to create a model with every space object? Why or why not?

___Possible answer: The nearest star and nearest galaxy will not fit in a model that shows the relative distances between the Sun and the planets.___

**Extension:** Create a model or drawing showing the relative diameters of the planets.

___The model or drawing should accurately demonstrate the relative diameters of the Sun and the planets.___

Decide which operation sign belongs in each box to make the number sentences true. You may need to use different operations more than once in each number sentence.

1. Operation signs: $+$, $-$, $\bullet$

   Number sentence: 12   4   6   3   7 = 37

   ___$12 \bullet 4 - 6 \bullet 3 + 7 = 37$___

2. Operation signs: $\div$, $+$, $-$

   Number sentence: 18   2   24   12   4 = 22

   ___$18 + 2 - 24 \div 4 = 22$___

# Recording Sheet for Reaching All Learners
## *Variables and Algebraic Expressions*

A magic square is an array of numbers in which each row, column, or diagonal has the same sum.

Decide if this is a magic square if $x = 4$, if $x = 6$, and if $x = 0$.

| | | |
|---|---|---|
| $x + 7$ | $x$ | $2x + 1$ |
| $x + 2$ | $0.5x + 6$ | $x + 6$ |
| $3x - 5$ | $3x$ | $x + 1$ |

This is a magic square when $x = 4$, but not when $x = 6$ or $0$.

128          **Holt Middle School Math   Course 2**

---

## 2-1 Exponents

## Warm Up

**Simplify.**

**1.** $2 \cdot 2 \cdot 2$  **8**

**2.** $3 \cdot 3 \cdot 3 \cdot 3$  **81**

**3.** $5 \cdot 5 \cdot 5$  **125**

**4.** $4 \cdot 4 \cdot 4$  **64**

**5.** $6 \cdot 6 \cdot 6 \cdot 6 \cdot 6$  **7,776**

## Problem of the Day

You have just installed a water pond in your backyard. You intend to place water lilies in the pond. According to the package a water lily doubles in size every day. From the time you install the first lily until the entire surface of the pond is covered will take 20 days. How long will it take for the pond to be half covered?   **19 days**

## Lesson Quiz

**Find each value.**

**1.** $7^3$  **343**

**2.** $6^3$  **216**

**3.** $3^4$  **81**

**4.** $8^5$  **32,768**

**Write each number using an exponent and the given base.**

**5.** 125, base 5  $5^3$

**6.** 16, base 2  $2^4$

**7.** Find the volume of a cube if each side is 12 inches long.
  **1,728 in$^3$**

## 2-2 Powers of Ten and Scientific Notation

## Warm Up

**Find each value.**

**1.** $9^2$   81

**2.** $12^2$   144

**3.** $15^2$   225

**4.** $10^2$   100

**5.** $10^3$   1,000

**6.** $10^4$   10,000

## Problem of the Day

Each day, Lowell runs one more lap than he did the day before. At the end of one week he has run 77 laps. How many laps did he run on the first day?   **8**

## Lesson Quiz

**Multiply.**

**1.** $25 \times 10^2$   **2,500**

**2.** $18 \times 10^4$   **180,000**

**Find each product.**

**3.** $110 \times 10^2$   **11,000**

**4.** $3.742 \times 10^3$   **3,742**

**Write each number in scientific notation.**

**5.** 7,400,000   **$7.4 \times 10^6$**

**6.** 45,000   **$4.5 \times 10^4$**

**7.** Earth is about $9.292 \times 10^7$ miles from the Sun. Write this number in standard form.   **92,920,000**

## 2-3 Order of Operations

## Warm Up
**Evaluate in order from left to right.**

**1.** $18 \div 3 + 7$ **13**

**2.** $10^2 \div 4 - 8$ **17**

**3.** $10 + 23 - 8 + 7$ **32**

**4.** $8 \times 2 - 3 + 24$ **37**

**5.** $81 \div 9 \times 3 + 15$ **42**

## Problem of the Day
**Classify each statement as true or false. If the statement is false, insert parentheses to make it true.**

**1.** $4 \times (5 + 6) = 44$ **false**

**2.** $(24 - 4) \times 2 = 40$ **false**

**3.** $25 \div 5 + 6 \times 3 = 23$ **true**

**4.** $14 - 2^2 \div 2 = 12$ **true**

## Lesson Quiz
**Evaluate.**

**1.** $27 + 56 \div 7$ **35**

**2.** $9 \cdot 7 - 5$ **58**

**3.** $(28 - 8) \div 4$ **5**

**4.** $136 - 10^2 \div 5$ **116**

**5.** $(9 - 5)^3 \cdot (7 + 1)^2 \div 4$ **1,024**

**6.** Denzel paid a basic fee of $35 per month plus $2 for each phone call beyond his basic plan. Evaluate $35 + 8(2)$ to find out how much Denzel paid for a month with 8 calls outside of the basic plan. **$51**

# 2-4 Prime Factorization

## Warm Up

Write each number as a product of two whole numbers in as many ways as possible.

**1.** 6   $1 \cdot 6, 2 \cdot 3$

**2.** 16   $1 \cdot 16, 2 \cdot 8, 4 \cdot 4$

**3.** 17   $1 \cdot 17$

**4.** 36   $1 \cdot 36, 2 \cdot 18, 3 \cdot 12,$
$4 \cdot 9, 6 \cdot 6$

**5.** 23   $1 \cdot 23$

## Problem of the Day

Nicholas bikes every third day and skates every other day. Today is April 5, and Nicholas biked and skated. On what date will he both bike and skate?   **April 11**

## Lesson Quiz

Use a factor tree to find the prime factorization.

**1.** 27   $3^3$

**2.** 36   $2^2 \cdot 3^2$

**3.** 28   $2^2 \cdot 7$

Use a step diagram to find the prime factorization.

**4.** 132   $2^2 \cdot 3 \cdot 11$

**5.** 52   $2^2 \cdot 13$

**6.** 108   $2^2 \cdot 3^3$

## 2-5 Greatest Common Factor

## Warm Up
Write the prime factorization of each number.

**1.** 20   $2^2 \cdot 5$         **2.** 100   $2^2 \cdot 5^2$

**3.** 30   $2 \cdot 3 \cdot 5$        **4.** 128   $2^7$

**5.** 70   $2 \cdot 5 \cdot 7$

## Problem of the Day
Use the clues to find the numbers being described.

**1. a.** The greatest common factor (GCF) of two numbers is 5.

   **b.** The sum of the numbers is 75.

   **c.** The difference between the numbers is 5.   **35 and 40**

**2. a.** The GCF of three different numbers is 4.

   **b.** The sum of the numbers is 64.   **Possible answer: 12, 16, 36**

## Lesson Quiz
Find the greatest common factor (GCF).

**1.** 28, 40   **4**              **2.** 24, 56   **8**

**3.** 54, 99   **9**              **4.** 20, 35, 70   **5**

**5.** The math clubs from 3 schools agreed to a competition. Members from each club must be divided into teams, and teams from all clubs must be equally sized. What is the greatest number of members that can be on a team if Georgia has 16 members, Williams has 24 members and Fulton has 72 members?   **8**

## 2-6 Least Common Multiple

## Warm Up

**Write the prime factorization of each number.**

**1.** 68   $2^2 \cdot 17$

**2.** 225   $3^2 \cdot 5^2$

**3.** 940   $2^2 \cdot 5 \cdot 47$

**Find the greatest common factor.**

**4.** 27 and 45   **9**

**5.** 32 and 80   **16**

**6.** 50 and 71   **1**

## Problem of the Day

Franklin had some counters. When he counted them by twos, threes, fours, and fives, he had one left over. If Franklin had more than 100 and fewer than 150 counters, how many did he have?   **121**

## Lesson Quiz

**Find the least common multiple (LCM).**

**1.** 18, 21   **126**

**2.** 24, 27   **216**

**3.** 4, 6, 15   **60**

**4.** 4, 8, 16   **16**

**5.** You are planning a picnic. You can purchase paper plates in packages of 30, paper napkins in packages of 50, and paper cups in packages of 20. What is the least number of each type of package that you can buy and have an equal number of each?   **10 packages of plates, 6 packages of napkins, 15 packages of cups**

## 2-7 Variables and Algebraic Expressions

## Warm Up

**Evaluate.**

**1.** $5(7) - 1$ **34**

**2.** $7(18 - 11)$ **49**

**3.** $22 + 17 \times 8 + 3$ **161**

**4.** $36 + 15(40 - 35)$ **111**

**5.** $3^3 + 7(12 - 4)$ **83**

## Problem of the Day

How much will it cost to cut a log into eight pieces if cutting it into four pieces costs $12? **$28**

## Lesson Quiz

**Evaluate $n + 7$ for each value of $n$.**

**1.** $n = 25$ **32**

**2.** $n = 31$ **38**

**Evaluate each algebraic expression for the given values of the variables.**

**3.** $6y - 5$ for $y = 7$ **37**

**4.** $4x^2 + 3x$ for $x = 6$ **162**

**5.** $\frac{56}{x} + 3y$ for $x = 4$ and $y = 3$ **23**

**6.** The expression $7d$ gives the number of days in $d$ weeks. Evaluate $7d$ for $d = 12$. How many days are in 12 weeks? **84**

## 2-8 Translate Words Into Math

## Warm Up

**Evaluate each algebraic expression for the given values of the variables.**

**1.** $7x + 4$ for $x = 6$   **46**

**2.** $8y - 22$ for $y = 9$   **50**

**3.** $12x + \dfrac{8}{y}$ for $x = 7$ and $y = 4$   **86**

**4.** $y + 3z$ for $y = 5$ and $z = 6$   **23**

## Problem of the Day

A farmer had some ducks and cows in the field. He sent his two children out to count the number of animals. Jean counted 50 heads. Charles counted 154 legs. How many of each kind were counted?   **23 ducks and 27 cows**

## Lesson Quiz

**Write each phrase as an algebraic expression.**

**1.** 18 less than a number   $x - 18$

**2.** the quotient of a number and 21   $\dfrac{x}{21}$

**3.** 8 times the sum of $x$ and 15   $8(x + 15)$

**4.** 7 less than the product of a number and 5   $5n - 7$

**5.** The county fair charges an admission of $6 and then $2 for each ride. Write an algebraic expression to represent the total cost after $r$ rides at the fair.   $6 + 2r$

# 2-9 Combining Like Terms

## Warm Up

**Evaluate each expression for $y = 3$.**

**1.** $3y + y$   **12**

**2.** $7y$   **21**

**3.** $10y - 4y$   **18**

**4.** $9y$   **27**

**5.** $y + 5y + 6y$   **36**

**6.** $10y$   **30**

## Problem of the Day

Emilia saved nickels, dimes, and quarters in a jar. When the jar was full, she counted the money. She had as many quarters as dimes, but twice as many nickels as dimes. If the jar had 844 coins, how much money had she saved?   **$94.95**

## Lesson Quiz

**Identify like terms.**

**1.** $3n^2$  $5n$  $2n^3$  $8n$   **$5n, 8n$**

**2.** $a^5$  $2a^2$  $a^3$  $3a$  $4a^2$   **$2a^2, 4a^2$**

**Combine like terms.**

**3.** $4a + 3b + 2a$   **$6a + 3b$**

**4.** $x^2 + 2y + 8x^2$   **$9x^2 + 2y$**

**5.** Write an expression for the perimeter of the given figure.   **$6x + 8y$**

$2x + 3y$

$x + y$ ▢ $x + y$

$2x + 3y$

# 2-10 Equations and Their Solutions

## Warm Up

**Evaluate each expression for $x = 12$.**

**1.** $x + 2$    **14**

**2.** $\frac{x}{4}$    **3**

**3.** $x - 8$    **4**

**4.** $10x - 4$    **116**

**5.** $2x - 12$    **36**

**6.** $5x + 7$    **67**

## Problem of the Day

Alicia buys buttons at a cost of 8 for $20. She in turn resells them in her shop for $5 each. How many buttons does Alicia need to sell in order to make a profit of $120?    **48 buttons**

## Lesson Quiz

**Determine if each number is a solution of $5 + x = 47$.**

**1.** $x = 42$    **yes**

**2.** $x = 52$    **no**

**Determine if each number is a solution of $57 - y = 18$.**

**3.** $y = 75$    **no**

**4.** $y = 39$    **yes**

**5.** Kwan has 14 marbles. This is 7 more than Drue has. Does Drue have 21 or 7 marbles?    **7**

# 2-11 Solving Equations by Adding or Subtracting

## Warm Up

Determine if the given numbers are solutions of the given equations.

**1.** $y = 9$ for $y - 8 = 1$   **yes**   **2.** $x = 2$ for $4x = 9$   **no**

**3.** $x = 5$ for $8x + 2 = 42$   **yes** **4.** $x = 15$ for $7(x - 5) = 70$ **yes**

**5.** $x = 4$ for $3(x - 2) = 10$   **no**

## Problem of the Day

Four couples have dinner together each month. The wives are Ginny, Helen, Sarah and Bridget. The husbands are Mark, Alex, Stephen and Henry. Who is married to whom?

• Sarah is Mark's sister.

• Sarah introduced Henry to his wife.

• Bridget has 2 brothers, but her husband is an only child.

• Ginny is married to Stephen.

**Ginny and Stephen, Helen and Mark, Sarah and Alex, Bridget and Henry**

## Lesson Quiz

Solve each equation. Check your answer.

**1.** $x - 9 = 4$   $x = 13$          **2.** $y + 6 = 72$   $y = 66$

**3.** $21 = n - 41$   $n = 62$          **4.** $127 = w + 31$   $w = 96$

**5.** $81 = x - 102$   $x = 183$

**6.** Tamika has sold 16 dozen cookies this week. This was 7 dozen more than she sold last week. Write and solve an equation to find how many dozen cookies she sold last week.
$x + 7 = 16$; **9 dozen**

## 2-12 Solving Equations by Multiplying or Dividing

## Warm Up

**Solve.**

**1.** $x + 5 = 9$  **$x = 4$**
 **2.** $x - 34 = 72$  **$x = 106$**

**3.** $124 = x - 39$  **$x = 163$**

## Problem of the Day

What 4-digit number am I?  **4,039**

• I am greater than 4,000 and less than 5,000.

• The sum of my hundreds digit and my ones digit is 9.

• Twice my tens digit is 2 more than my thousands digit.

• The product of my hundreds digit and my ones digit is 0.

• I am not an even number.

## Lesson Quiz

**Solve the equation. Check your answer.**

**1.** $12 = 4x$  **$x = 3$**
  **2.** $18z = 90$  **$z = 5$**

**3.** $12 = \frac{x}{4}$  **$x = 48$**
  **4.** $840 = 12y$  **$y = 70$**

**5.** $\frac{h}{22} = 9$  **$h = 198$**

**6.** The cost of each ticket at the carnival was $0.25. Li bought $7.50 worth of tickets. How many tickets did she buy?  **30**